30/11

Pub. 2011

The Russian Court at Sea

The Russian Court at Sea

The voyage of
HMS *Marlborough*, April 1919

FRANCES WELCH

First published in 2011 by

Short Books
3A Exmouth House
Pine Street
EC1R 0JH

10 9 8 7 6 5 4 3 2

All extracts from the Dowager Empress Marie's diaries are printed from the
original Danish publication – *Kejsevinde Dagmars Fangenskab Paa Krim*,
edited by Preben Ulstrup, (2005) – courtesy of Gyldendal, Denmark

A CIP catalogue record for this book is available from the British Library.

ISBN 978-1-906021-78-8

Printed in Great Britain by Clays, Suffolk

Lula and Silas

The Voyage of HMS *Marlborough*, April 1919

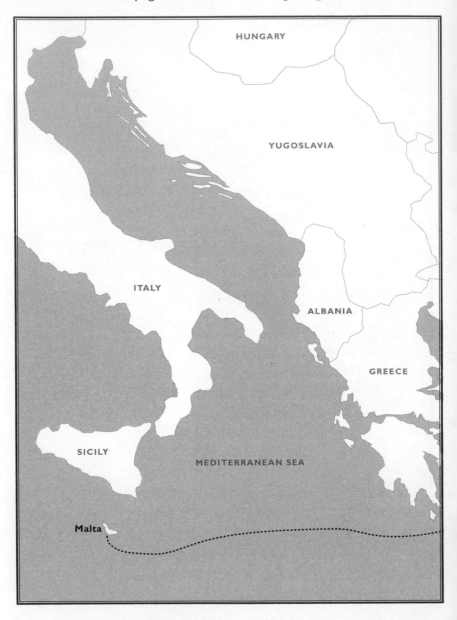

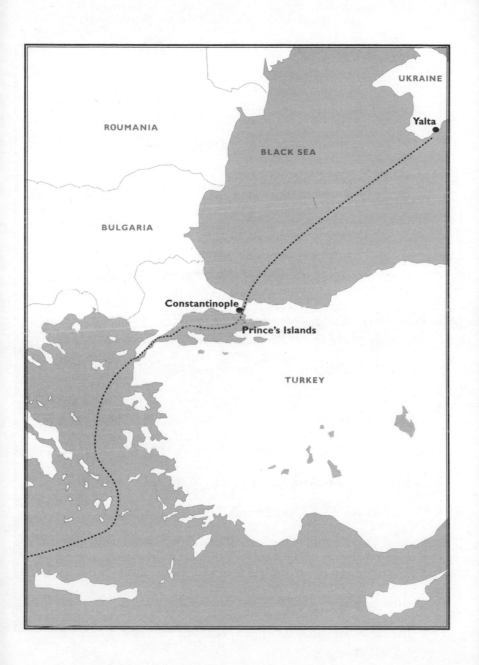

DRAMATIS PERSONAE

The Ai-Todors

The Dowager Empress Marie Feodorovna,
mother of the Tsar 1847-1928

Grand Duchess Xenia, *sister of the Tsar 1875-1960*

Prince Dmitri, *grandson of the Tsar, son of Grand Duchess Xenia*
1901-1980

Prince Vassily, *grandson of the Tsar, son of Grand Duchess Xenia*
1907-1989

Princess Irina, *granddaughter of the Tsar, daughter of Grand*
Duchess Xenia and wife of Prince Felix Youssoupov 1895-1970

Prince Felix Youssoupov, *murderer of Rasputin 1887-1967*

The Dulbers

Grand Duke Nicholas, *or Nikolasha, cousin of the Tsar 1856-1929*

Grand Duchess Anastasia, *wife of Nikolasha 1868-1935*

Grand Duke Peter, *brother of Nikolasha 1864-1931*

Grand Duchess Militsa, *wife of Grand Duke Peter 1866-1951*

Princess Marina, *daughter of Peter and Militsa 1892-1981*

Prince Roman, *son of Peter and Militsa 1896-1978*

Princess Nadezhda, *daughter of Peter and Militsa, wife of Nicholas*
Orloff, 1898-1988

Further Passengers

Prince Felix Youssoupov (sen), *Felix's father, former Governor of Moscow* 1856-1928

Princess Zenaide Youssoupov, *Felix's mother* 1861-1939

Princess Sofka Dolgorouky (later Skipwith), *granddaughter of the Dowager's best friend, Baroness Dolgorouky* 1907-1994

Prince Nicholas Orloff, 1891-1961

Prince Serge Dolgorouky, *equerry to the Dowager* 1872-1933

Countess Zenaide Mengden, *Empress's lady-in-waiting,* 1878-1950

Princess Aprak Obolensky, *Empress's lady-in-waiting,* 1851-1943

Miss Henton, *or Henty, governess and nanny to the Youssoupovs* 1866-1940

Miss Coster, *or Nana Coster, governess and nanny to Grand Duchess Xenia's children*

Miss King, *governess to the Dolgoroukys*

Officers

Captain Charles Johnson 1869-1930

Commander Henry 'Tom' Fothergill 1881-1963

First Lieutenant Francis Pridham 1886-1975

April 7th, 1919

As the light of a brilliant Crimean day began to fade, a picturesque group gathered on the beach below the imposing estate of Koreiz. At its heart were 17 members of the Russian Imperial Family and their entourages, including five small children, six dogs and a canary.

Among the principal Romanovs were the Tsar's mother, the Dowager Empress Marie, and his sister, the Grand Duchess Xenia. The resemblance between mother and daughter was immediately obvious; both had an air of defiance about them, evident in everything from the way they stood to their strong facial features.

Once crowned Tsarina of all the Russias, the elder woman now rejected all flamboyance in her dress; she and her daughter both chose to wear inconspicuous, dark clothes. Later that evening, the pair would walk the decks of a British battleship unrecognised and unnoticed. Their identity would emerge only when the mortified officer in charge noted a further likeness: the Dowager greatly resembled her sister, England's Queen Alexandra.

The Dowager and her daughter, clutching her pet dog Toby, were among the last to make their way to an ornate jetty. Both were struggling with their emotions. The Dowager later described their feelings: 'What grief and desperation'... 'Poor Xenia was weeping dreadfully.'

Prior to the arrival of the two women, the group had been dominated by the Tsar's 'dread uncle', the colossal Grand Duke Nicholas. The Grand Duke, former Commander of the Russian Army, seemed to make a point of staking his claim as first at the quay. In dramatic, almost aggressive, contrast to the women, his appearance was eye-catching and intimidating. He stood, an imposing six feet seven, in full traditional Cossack military uniform, with Circassian coat and medals.

He was accompanied by his reedy brother, Grand Duke Peter. This younger Grand Duke distanced himself from his brother's war-mongering appearance, preferring conventional Edwardian clothes, glasses and a deer-stalker hat. Beside him stood two of his three children: the ascetic-looking Prince Roman, 22, and cheery Princess Marina, 27.

The two Grand Dukes were accompanied by their wives, both Princesses of Montenegro, known jointly as 'the Black Peril'. The brothers' contrasting proportions were reflected in their choice of sisters: Grand Duke Nicholas's wife's face was as round and robust as her sister's was long and drawn.

Hardly less captivating, at some distance from the Grand Dukes and their entourages, stood members of Russia's wealthiest family: the Youssoupovs. Prince Felix Youssoupov, a nephew by marriage of the Tsar, was best known as the man who had killed the controversial holy man Rasputin.

This fabled murderer also had a reputation for flamboyance, so he might have disappointed onlookers with his plain trilby and lightweight belted coat. But there was no disguising his elegant stature and remarkable good looks. The Prince had delicate facial features: slightly hooded eyes and a small mouth, frequently crimped at the corners in a brazen grin.

His father, meanwhile, the elder Prince Felix Youssoupov, had chosen to match the Grand Duke Nicholas in full, arresting Cossack military costume. While the elder Prince could not boast a distinguished war record, he was perhaps mindful of his position as owner of this particular *mise en scène*. The grandeur and savagery of his costume echoed the mood of the Koreiz estate, where sumptuous buildings pitted themselves against the encroaching Tartar wilderness. From its splendid terraces could occasionally be discerned the estate village, in which braying donkeys vied with the Moslem call to prayer.

The rough, winding road to the beach of Koreiz was now alive with motorcars and horse-drawn carriages. It is hard to know what each new arrival would have made of their first sight of the British battleship HMS *Marlborough*. The ship loomed majestically a little way offshore and all but the very youngest members of the party understood that they must embark within hours.

The Tsar's 11-year-old nephew, Prince Vassily, often recalled his excitement as he contemplated travelling aboard a warship. But for many of the older members of the party, the sight could only serve to remind them that, while they finally knew by what means they would leave their homeland, they still had no fixed destination.

Some wistfully savoured what they feared would be their last views of the Tartar landscape. Their gaze would have been caught by the Youssoupovs' statue of Minerva presiding over the jetty. They may also have ventured a final look at the bronze of 'Terzy', a mythical Tartar gypsy said to have thrown herself in the sea after being kidnapped by pirates. Others of the party were perhaps silently thanking God that, at last, they were leaving. They had suffered two turbulent

The Koreiz estate house; and below,
the statue of Minerva presiding over the jetty

years since the Revolution. Within the last nine months, 17 members of the Imperial Family had been murdered. On the night of July 16th/17th, 1918 the Tsar, Tsarina and their five children had been killed in Ekaterinburg. The following night, the Tsarina's sister had been buried alive, thrown down a mine with five other Romanovs.

Watching from some distance were several of the *Marlborough*'s officers. They had supervised the successful construction of a makeshift pier from which small boats would transport the party to the ship. But the men's satisfaction with the intricate pier soon gave way to irresistible fascination with the plight of their prospective passengers. The *Marlborough*'s First Lieutenant, Francis Pridham, was overwhelmed: 'It is dreadful to see them dazed and heartbroken except the younger ones who fortunately do not realise what is happening. Most of them have come at an hour's notice.'

The more stolid Commander Henry 'Tom' Fothergill described the scene in a letter to his sister, 'a whole crowd of Princes and Princesses about 30 with 42 servants and stacks of gear...' His conclusion was curiously enthusiastic: 'We are having a great show here – a little too strenuous from my point of view. But I wouldn't have missed it for worlds.'

In the grip of heightened emotion, these beleaguered members of the Imperial Family would surely have derived comfort from at least being together. But there was at this time considerable tension within the family, the result of a power struggle which had been reignited by recent events, the source of which went back many years.

Grand Duke Nicholas's warlike demeanour, which so impressed the British officers, was actually exacerbated by a fit of pique – caused by an earlier slight from the Dowager.

Happily, the officers were not quibbling: 'a magnificent-looking man', breathed Pridham, 'an almost awe-inspiring presence'. He was particularly struck by the Grand Duke's lambskin Astrakhan hat which, he felt, accentuated the Grand Duke's great height. Fothergill was equally taken, though characteristically less expansive: 'a very tall thin man, one of the best of the Russian family.'

Neither officer could have imagined that the Grand Duke, once master of the million-strong Russian Army, had experienced mortifying difficulties bringing his relations into line. The evening's arrangements had begun badly when he sent a message to the Dowager instructing her to pack and to be ready at his brother's estate, by 4.45pm. The Dowager did not like the instruction, which gave her less than two and a half hours to pack. Nor did she like the way in which it was delivered. As she exclaimed: '*Qu'est-ce qu'il a, le grand duc?*'

The Grand Duke's messenger later left an account of the exchange: 'She was terribly angry, called the Allies "*cochons*" and complained with unflattering words that they had not given her time to pack as she wanted to... I said the Grand Duke had waited for the last opportunity, but now he had received information from two sides that it is essential to leave. She had retorted that she would come at 5.00 and not a minute earlier.' In the end she was 45 minutes late. By the time she arrived at his brother's estate, the Grand Duke was frantic with worry. He had eventually sent a car to her estate to find out what had happened.

Upon her arrival at the beach, the Dowager was at pains to appear unrushed. She would readily cross the beach with her daughter Xenia and her five sorrowful grandsons: the boys had all packed small bags of earth as mementos of their estate. But not before carrying out a series of elaborate farewell gestures. The messenger who had witnessed her earlier outburst watched his 'beloved sovereign' with anguish. 'On the way the Empress gave her hand to the officers, who kissed it with respect... To see how the Empress Maria left Russian soil was enough to make you weep. I could not withold my tears and cried.'

One of the marines from the *Marlborough*, William 'Bill' Phillips, never forgot the sight. 'On arriving at the beach she – the Dowager – descended from the landau, shook hands with the coachman, kissed one of the leading ponies, turned and walked down to the boat. A brave lady.'

She later unburdened her feelings in her diary, particularly bemoaning her damaged pride: 'to be driven away like a criminal... like a knock on the head'.

On completion of her stately journey to the *Marlborough*, one of her first acts was to take the principal Allied '*cochon*' to task: 'I misbehaved toward Captain Johnson by complaining about how everything had been arranged. He only answered that it had all been necessary and that he had delayed the departure until the last minute.'

In periods of great danger, petty irritations can become a sort of refuge. The time had come, it seemed, for the embattled Romanovs to relinquish annoyances and acknowledge the graver aspects of their terrible predicament. The Bolsheviks were now perilously close and presented a mortal threat. On April 6th, the *Marlborough* ship's log recorded 'continuous rifle fire from the shore'.

~·~

The closing months of 1905 had proved fateful ones for the

last Tsar Nicholas II of Russia. On November 1st he wrote in his diary: 'We had tea with Militsa and Stana. We met the man of God Grigory from the province of Tobol.' The bald entry marks the momentous introduction of the Imperial couple to Rasputin by the Montenegrin sisters or Black Peril, the Grand Duchesses Militsa and Anastasia.

The beautiful Montenegrin Princesses were known as the Black Peril partly because of their dark hair but mostly because of their predilection for mystics. They had come to the Russian Court under the Dowager Empress's protection. She had initially approved of them, arranging the elder sister Militsa's marriage to Grand Duke Peter and Anastasia's marriage to a more obscure Romanov cousin.

But the Dowager soon found the sisters too much for her. By the early 1900s they were introducing the Tsar and Tsarina to a series of mystics. The most successful of these, a Frenchman, promised to help provide an heir for the Imperial couple, who had had their fourth daughter in 1900. The Dowager, with her feet firmly on the ground, was so alarmed that she launched a formal inquiry into this particular mystic's background. She was not impressed by tales that he could control the weather or make people invisible.

The family feuds multiplied. The younger of the Dowager's protégées, Anastasia, staged a separate coup by embarking on an affair with the powerful Grand Duke Nicholas. Princess Anastasia had chosen well: by 1905, the Grand Duke would have been one of the most important men in Russia.

Such had been the Grand Duke's power that, shortly before the fateful tea, he had been called upon to set himself up as a military dictator. This, however, he had loyally refused to do, pronouncing, with characteristic dash, that if he was forced into such a position he would shoot himself in front of the Tsar.

The Dowager, then in Denmark, would have appreciated the Grand Duke's shows of allegiance to her son but she remained mistrustful of his power. In a bid to denigrate his growing popular appeal, she denounced him as 'sick with an incurable illness – he's a fool.'

However, her mistrust of the Grand Duke proved as nothing compared to her loathing for the Black Peril's new mystic, Rasputin. The Dowager watched in horror as, after 1905, Rasputin swiftly established himself at Court, soothing her neurotic daughter-in-law, the Tsarina, and apparently healing her haemophiliac grandson, the Tsarevich Alexis. As introducers of this evil to the Court, the Montenegrin Princesses were well on the way to earning the Dowager's nickname for them: 'cockroaches'.

Happily for the Dowager, within just two years of introducing Rasputin to the Court, the sisters had fallen from grace. By the time the Tsar granted the Grand Duke permission to marry Anastasia, in 1907, Rasputin was refusing to visit either sister. Notwithstanding all his own peccadillos, Rasputin had apparently taken it upon himself to disapprove of Anastasia's divorce. Yet more disastrously for the sisters, the Tsar and Tsarina had decided to follow his lead. That same year, a furious Militsa retaliated, contributing to a file accusing Rasputin of False Doctrine and 'group sinning'.

The sisters' falling out with Rasputin might have scored them points with the Dowager but, sadly for them, more points were lost with the announcement of Anastasia's marriage to the Grand Duke. The Dowager was furious with her son for granting the couple permission to marry, not least because the match broke ecclesiastical ruling on marriage between brothers and sisters. She wrote a strong letter and took several tranquilising drops.

By the time the First World War broke out, hostility was so rife at the Russian Court that it could never be assumed that an enemy's enemy was a friend. The Dowager remained disconcerted by the Grand Duke's increasing popularity, not least when, in June 1915, a crowd stormed the Duma demanding he take power. She was no less worried by the continuing rise of Rasputin, who was now influencing the Tsar's choice of ministers.

But if these two were united by the Dowager's disapproval, they were not in any other respect allied. Grand Duke Nicholas may have been initially impressed by his wife's protégé, but by the time he took control of the Russian Army, he was infuriated by him. Indeed when Rasputin suggested he give a blessing to the Army at the front line, the Grand Duke's response was decisive: 'Come and I'll hang you.'

Rasputin fought back. Two months after the storming of the Duma, Grand Duke Nicholas was stripped of his role as Commander in Chief of the Army and sent to the Caucasus. The Tsar then, controversially, put himself at the head of the Army. A letter from the Tsarina to the Tsar makes it quite clear who was behind the Grand Duke's dismissal. She refers to Rasputin as 'Our Friend' and the Tsar, confusingly, as 'he': 'Our Friend says that... if he had not taken the place of Nikolai Nikolaievich (the Grand Duke) he would now be thrown off the throne.' Rasputin would later boast that he had 'sunk' the unfortunate Grand Duke.

The Dowager was horrified by this development. While she did not mind seeing the Grand Duke rebutted, she could imagine the dire consequences of the Tsar putting himself at the head of a struggling army. Worse, she realised that, with the Tsar at the front, the Tsarina and Rasputin would be left in charge of the Government. Redoubling her efforts to rid the Court of Rasputin, she and Xenia now went to Tsarskoe Selo to talk to the Tsarina. On August 31st, she wrote: 'With Xenia to Tsarskoe Selo to try my luck... Drank tea with Alicky, who spoke about everything except what exercises me the most.'

In exasperation, the Dowager decided to leave St Petersburg for good in early 1916, settling instead in Kiev. According to Felix Youssoupov, the Dowager gave her son an ultimatum: 'Either me or Rasputin.'

The turmoil created by the continuing presence of Rasputin at Court meant that his murder became almost inevitable. The killing was finally carried out in the cellar of the Moika Palace in St Petersburg, in December 1916, by Youssoupov, Prince Dmitri Romanov and a member of the Duma, Vladimir Purishkevich. There were conflicting tales of their struggles to shoot, poison and finally drown the so-called holy man.

When the Dowager heard of his death she was uneasy; as a devout Christian, she could never condone murder. Other members of the Imperial Family had no such qualms, simply organising a petition to appeal for clemency towards the murderers. In the end, although the Tsar was obdurate – 'a murder is always a murder' – the punishments were not severe: Youssoupov was exiled to one of his estates, and Prince Dmitri to Persia, while Purishkevich remained entirely unpunished. The Dowager herself soon cast aside her misgivings, electing to visit Youssoupov with his wife, her granddaughter Irina.

Within months of Rasputin's murder, the country was engulfed in revolution and the Tsar had abdicated. The

Dowager was devastated, repeatedly referring to the abdication as 'the greatest humiliation of my life'. She wrote in her diary: 'Am completely disconsolate!! To think that I should live to witness such horror... I am in despair over everything.'

She was stunned by the Romanovs' swift downfall. The Provisional Government produced a special decree prohibiting members of the Romanov family from further service in the Army or Navy. Grand Duke Nicholas, his brother Grand Duke Peter and his nephew, Prince Roman all offered their help to the Tsar as he faced his abdication crisis. The same day that the three were told of the special decree – March 11th 1917 – the Romanovs, in high dudgeon, resigned their oaths of allegiance to the Provisional Government.

Xenia's three eldest sons had also attempted, with Youssoupov, to join the White Army. All four had been rejected: deemed again, as disgraced Romanovs, 'undesirable'.

Meanwhile, in Kiev the Dowager was exposed to hostile graffiti: 'Romanovs, the enemies of the Revolution and the Russian people.' By the beginning of April 1917, the new authorities were ordering her to leave for the relative safety of the Crimea.

Various members of the Imperial Family had bought up land in the Crimea on the Black Sea coast. These estates comprised, first, the Tsar's grand palace at Livadia; at some distance stood Ai-Todor, owned by Grand Duchess Xenia and, next but one, Dulber, owned by Grand Duke Peter.

The Dowager spent most of her time at Ai-Todor with Xenia. Nikolasha, meanwhile, had his own estate, Tchair, which some time after the Dowager's arrival in the Crimea, he was obliged to sell up and leave. He and his wife Anastasia then moved to Dulber. Thus the principal Romanov households were established and became known, at least to the Dowager, as the 'Ai-Todors' and the 'Dulbers'.

The Ai-Todors comprised the Dowager, Xenia, her husband Grand Duke Alexander, and their six sons. Honorary Ai-Todors included Felix Youssoupov and his wife Irina, and their baby, also called Irina. Youssoupovs' parents, the elder Prince Felix, who took such pride in his Cossack uniform, and the former beauty Princess Zenaide, were close friends of the Dowager and would also have considered themselves Ai-Todors.

The Dulbers, meanwhile, consisted of Grand Duke Nicholas, who despite not owning the estate, remained its undisputed head, the more retiring Grand Duke Peter, and the Black Peril. Peter and Militsa had three children: Nadezhda, who married during the exile and moved to a house nearby, her elder sister Marina and brother Roman. After the Montenegrins' fall from grace at Court, Dulber inevitably became a sort of *salon des refusés*. But these long years in the wilderness did nothing to lower the spirits of at least two of their children: the friendly Marina and the good-hearted Roman.

During their two years in the Crimea, the Ai-Todors had as little to do with the Dulbers as they possibly could. Xenia and Militsa made much of tending roses on their respective estates. The younger Ai-Todors spent months at a time running wild about the grounds, riding, hunting and fishing. Vassily always remembered being torn between partings as he was obliged, upon leaving, to hand his bicycle over to his tutor and say goodbye to his favourite pony. The fourth son Dmitri, who was not as robust as his brothers, established a cooking chalet.

But all the estates suffered raids and severe food restrictions were imposed. Soon after the Dowager's arrival, in the spring of 1917, government restrictions were enforced on movement. Youssoupov, his wife Irina and Grand Duke Nicholas's doctor, who were not classified as Romanovs, were the only three allowed to travel between the estates. These three were able to keep the lines of communication open between the Dowager and the Grand Duke Nicholas. But whether the Dowager wanted to hear news of Grand Duke Nicholas, Grand Duke Peter and the Black Peril was another matter.

After the Bolshevik Revolution, the exiles' situation became more perilous. In the end, anxious about threats from more aggressive Bolshevik factions, their guard insisted the Ai-Todors move to Dulber. He selected Dulber because it was surrounded by high walls. Perhaps for reasons of diplomacy, the Dowager was not kept fully abreast of the controversial plan; up until the last minute she was under the impression that she was packing to return to St Petersburg. The plan created no less alarm at Dulber; Roman later wrote that until then he had not seen the Dowager for a full five years.

Her horror when she found herself at Dulber was such that, for several weeks, she refused to leave her new rooms. It was left to her uncharacteristically nervous hostess, Grand Duchess Militsa, to break the ice. Militsa contrived to visit the Dowager every afternoon, ostensibly to ask her guest if she needed anything.

Fortunately for all the captives, the Germans were awarded the Crimea in a separate peace. With the arrival of the new German rulers, in April 1918, the Dowager and fellow Ai-Todors were able to return to their own estate. There followed another hiatus, during which the Dulbers and Ai-Todors reverted to their separate rounds of tennis parties and picnics.

But following the Armistice in November, the Germans were ousted and the Bolsheviks came flooding back. Thoroughly alarmed, the British Government began serious efforts to get the Dowager out of Russia. The Dowager was reluctant to leave. Her preoccupation with her personal humiliation matched her anxiety not to be seen to be abandoning her people.

Among the first plans the Dowager rejected was a secret rescue, to be carried out on a small boat under cover of darkness. Commander Charles Turle reported in a secret memo on Nov 22nd, 1918: 'I am of the opinion that Her Majesty, unless actually attacked, will certainly not leave the Crimea except openly and in a large vessel, and then only if order has been restored, either by the Allies or by a local Government.'

The Dowager's sister, Queen Alexandra, became increasingly worried. Just before Christmas 1918, she sent an urgent letter through the Royal Navy communications system: 'Darling Minny have just been informed that it would be most advisable for you to leave at once before more complications and horrors so please make up your mind before too late to come to me here in England at once. Bring everybody you wish, your loving sister Alix.'

The Dowager's reply was dismissive: 'Darling Alix, thank you with all my heart for your dear telegram. Though I long to see you awfully, see no real necessity to leave now for the moment. Have written today. Loving Christmas wishes to you all. Your loving sister Minny.'

But the danger intensified and the pressure to leave became ever more urgent. The Dowager may now have begun weighing up some thorny logistics. With the Romanovs' increasing isolation, she would have recognised the growing likelihood of the Ai-Todors and Dulbers being forced together. If the Ai-Todors left, would the Dulbers also have to leave? Would they all have to leave together?

Turle's envoy visited several times through January. In February, another naval officer, Leslie Ashmore, was promised petrol to get to Yalta for his honeymoon if he delivered letters to the Dowager. But on March 19 a telegram sent from the Black Sea to the Admiralty contained a simple message: 'Empress declines to leave.'

Finally King George V, the Dowager's nephew, weighed in, instructing the Admiralty to send a message to the Commander in Chief in the Mediterranean: 'His Majesty expresses great concern for the personal safety of Empress Marie and other members of Russian Royal Family now in Crimea. Admiralty considers situation is now such that they should be embarked whatever may be their personal desires and removed to a place of safety as soon as preparations can be made.'

The *Marlborough* officers were in no doubt as to the awkwardness of their situation. Commander Fothergill retained a stark naval signal addressed to him: 'Our job is to stand by to evacuate the Empress Dowager and suite of about 70 persons if she can be persuaded to leave!!!'

The two hours Captain Johnson spent with the Dowager were doubtless uncomfortable for them both; he was not interested in being charming, still less in being courtly. As First Lieutenant Pridham later said : 'She refused to come on board in answer to her sister's letter until we promised that we would put in safety all the loyal people in that area of the Crimea, and there were hundreds of them.'

It must have been clear to the Dowager by then that the

Ai-Todors and Dulbers would have to leave together. Her solicitude for her fellow refugees may have been prompted by the thought that, without her interference, her sole companions on the journey into exile would be her dreaded fellow Romanovs.

On April 7th, the Dowager, finally resigned to her fate, wrote: 'Today it is two years ago that we arrived here... At the time I thought that it would be just for a few months and that I would be able to go home to Petersburg: *"L'homme propose mais Dieu dispose".*'

~~~~~~~

It was to the *Marlborough*'s flurried First Lieutenant Pridham that the controversial arrangements fell. Fifty years later he still recalled his discomfort at realising he had been misinformed about numbers boarding. He had been told the ship was taking only the Empress and a small retinue of, as he put it, '12 personages from the Imperial Family'. Now he found himself faced with accommodating some 50 refugees. The *Marlborough* was a distingushed Iron Duke battleship still bearing the scars of a torpedo hit at Jutland in 1916. She was a man-of-war, entirely unequipped for passengers.

Pridham had set about freeing all 35 officers' cabins and putting up to three beds in each. It was still not enough: 'It turned out to be seven, I think, or eight, I can't remember the exact number now for which we had no special arrangement at all. We had no extra blankets or pillowcases or mattresses. So when we got to the stage of receiving these people on board we just had to rake up sheets from all the officers, and pillows and mattresses and put them on deck.' In his memoir, *En Exil*, Felix Youssoupov gives a colourful description of the accommodation: 'People slept everywhere on divans, hammocks or other "*lits de fortune*" sometimes even on the ground.'

Pridham, then aged 32, was considered undemonstrative and stiff by his family. But it is clear from his diary that he acknowledged the emotional gravity of his passengers' situation. As he wrote that evening: 'I cannot end my account of this first day of the embarkation without having mentioned the extraordinary fortitude shown by these people on their day of severance from their country. Though it seemed likely that the Empress Marie and those closest to her would go to England for a time, the destination for the remainder was not then known. Nevertheless their chief concern was to cause us as little inconvenience as possible.'

The tribute has a decorous, Edwardian flavour, but his beleaguered passengers would have been as grateful for decorum as they were for sympathy. Photographs taken aboard the *Marlborough* suggest that Pridham was master of both. He had a full mouth and strong jaw that protruded slightly; the firm chin and brow were softened by eyes that seem to narrow in a smile. His face has a kindly cast as he is pictured, during the voyage, listening attentively to the Dowager.

The more dour Captain Charles Johnson is unlikely to have shared Pridham's inclinations or emotions. Then aged 50, he was older than the other officers; he had enjoyed a distinguished naval career, sinking his first German submarine in 1915 and being awarded a DSO. He was inclined to keep his own counsel and in photographs looks slightly defensive and forbidding, with furtive eyes and a pursed mouth. There is none of the bearded bonhomie normally associated with naval captains.

Captain Johnson's father was a canon in the Church of Ireland; he had not had a particularly privileged upbringing, having been raised in a small vicarage in Carbury with nine jostling brothers; he would have had little time for Court etiquette. He had given up his quarters for the Dowager and would have felt no need for further generosity of spirit.

Giving up quarters was a considerable sacrifice; Captain Bligh is meant to have paved the way for the mutiny on the *Bounty* by allowing his airy rooms to be used for breadfruit plants. Quartered with the men, he lost his authority and within weeks was victim of a full-scale mutiny, put to sea in a rowing-boat.

The *Marlborough*'s Commander 'Tom' Fothergill, then 37, was also a bit chary about the irregularities of the *Marlborough*'s 'show'. A conscientious sailor and veteran of Jutland who had followed his father and elder brother into the services – both became colonels in the Royal Marines – Fothergill emerges from his early letters primarily as a friendly and cheerful man, offering brief but enthusiastic accounts of 'standing tiffins', parties and a girl 'who danced so rippingly'. He had a trustworthy face with fine features. In photographs there is a play about the mouth which makes him seem both humorous and tentative.

But in some respects he makes little of the Romanovs coming on board, not even attempting to distinguish one from the other. It is perhaps significant that the only figure he remarks upon initially is the Grand Duke Nicholas.

Pridham maintained that the Commander and Captain Johnson both had reservations about women and that neither would have relished the prospect of 38 female passengers boarding for an indefinite period. They may have subscribed to the traditional notion among sailors, that women on ships brought bad luck.

But First Lieutenant Pridham felt altogether differently. At this point he was the only one of the three most prominent officers who was married. He also had two daughters and thus had no doubts about his ability to look after any number of female passengers. As he wrote: 'Being First Lieutenant and therefore responsible for all questions of accommodation in the ship and both my Captain and Commander being misogynists, I was willingly handed the problem of not only arranging for their accommodation and means but also for their recreation and relaxation.'

He was perhaps overly critical. Whatever Fothergill's view may have been of women on ships, he was himself courting and would be married within a year. Any charge of misogyny would have been thrown out immediately by his fondest correspondents: a fleet of five sisters in Chobham. Captain Johnson's attitude, however, would be harder to gauge. He did marry late in life but his wife was, according to his

The *Marlborough*'s
Commander
'Tom' Fothergill

First Lieutenant Pridham, in later
years, and below, Captain Johnson

nephew, a woman 'of whom nobody seemed to approve'.

Pridham retreated to his cabin to write his diary, at some pains, with 'one finger of each hand'. 'I had my typewriter on the table in my cabin and whenever I had a minute or two to spare I went up and flicked off a few (notes).' His enthusiasm for all aspects of the *Marlborough*'s forthcoming adventure was unequivocal: 'There are four generations of Romanovs on board, I am sure no ship has ever before had a great grandmother on board with her daughter, grand-daughter and great granddaughter.'

Day 1

SHIP'S LOG APRIL 7:
15.30 BOATS EMPLOYED EMBARKING HIH EMPRESS
MARIE OF RUSSIA, ROYAL FAMILY AND LUGGAGE

It was the Grand Duke Nicholas and his fellow Dulbers who were the first to establish themselves on board. The Grand Duke, now aged 62, still cut a dash. In the early days after the Revolution, he had requested and been granted permission from the Provisional Government to continue wearing military uniform. He had been awarded the St George's Cross and a golden sword 'for valour'. He was not short of a sense of self-worth; indeed at one point he apparently hoped the Tsar would abdicate in favour of the 12-year-old Tsarevich and that he himself would be invited to act as regent until the boy reached his majority at 16.

Striking his first poses on the deck of the *Marlborough*, 'Nikolasha', as he was known, may have relished the thought of this new audience comparing him to his diminutive cousin, the Tsar. The Tsar, at five feet four, was self-conscious about his height and inclined to stand for long periods on tiptoe. Their meetings tended to begin badly: with Nikolasha entering the palace as if he were leading a cavalry charge, planting himself, Colossus-like before his cousin, then roaring, 'Good morning, Nicky'. At these moments the Tsar would surely have understood John Updike's description of one of his characters as 'insolently tall; as if he had just drawn himself up in a full-body sneer'.

As the Grand Duke now strode across the deck, the sailors' thoughts may have echoed those of enraptured courtiers describing his progress across the soft rugs of the palace: the swishing of his enormous feet would, apparently, fill the elegant halls with the free driving wind of the Asiatic steppes.

There were further tales of him intimidating his cavalry regiments. As his men galloped past him, he would beat his chest and twist his cap, finally ripping it to pieces. At the outset of the First World War, he had assembled his generals, then kept them waiting several hours before addressing them with these few words: 'You do your duty to the uttermost and I am with you: steal and I will hang you every one.'

Nicholas II had an understandably ambivalent attitude towards Nikolasha. Having first removed him from office, one of his last acts as Tsar was to try to reinstall him as Supreme Commander in Chief.

As the rest of the passengers boarded, mounting stairs lowered from two open gangways, the crew was able to savour first impressions of the Grand Duke's less exciting companions. His brother, the Grand Duke Peter, was among the early disappointments. Pridham felt the brothers resembled each other only in height. In fact, facially they were quite similar, with large, hooded eyes and generous noses. But Grand Duke Peter, at age 55, was significantly younger-looking, thinner and, crucially, went for the less

Grand Duke Nicholas, on deck on the *Marlborough; and* below, his brother about whom Pridham wrote dismissively: 'He was quite unlike his brother, and not in good health.'

imposing moustache without beard.

Throughout the war, Grand Duke Peter had worked under his brother as a general inspector of the Pioneer troops; he reached the rank of Lieutenant General and was Aide-de-Camp General to the Tsar. But unfortunately he had been forced into retirement by ill health. He was, in any case, a more sensitive, thoughtful type, interested in architecture and art. On one of his estates he had cultivated a fruit garden famed for its peaches and apricots. The impressionable Pridham was slightly dismissive; Grand Duke Peter, he wrote, was 'quite unlike his brother' and 'not in good health'.

The brothers' wives, the Black Princesses, now in their early fifties, were distinctly homely. What the crew made of them cannot be known, but Pridham's description showed characteristic gallantry. He described them as daughters of King Nicholas, 'that old fox', but added that they were considered 'in their day the two most beautiful women in Russia'. He gives no hint of the effects of the ravages of time. In fact, on the *Marlborough*, both former beauties appeared rather forbidding. While 50-year-old Anastasia's rounder face seemed to have crumpled into an expression of blustering impatience, her 52-year-old sister's long narrow face and drooping eyes had assumed an expression of sorrow.

Anastasia's fabled black hair was greying; she now appeared distinctly dumpy. However, she had never failed in her role as chatelaine of Grand Duke Nicholas's Crimean estate, Tchair, where she cultivated roses – to this day remembered in a passionate tango 'In Tchair Park the Roses Blossomed'.

Nor had she lost any of her spirit. A year before, Anastasia had given short shrift to a German general who arrived at Tchair politely requesting an interview with the Grand Duke Nicholas. Nikolasha flatly refused to see him; instead he sent his stout wife to the front gates, where she assailed the general with a broom.

Her elder but lesser-known sister, Militsa, had not only been a beauty; she spoke five languages and was deeply versed in the history of Orthodoxy. She had published a work of her own entitled *Selected Passages from the Holy Fathers* and was considered a prophetess by some at Court. Others were less convinced; one particularly damaging story concerned her claiming to be invisible solely because her companion wore a magic hat.

Militsa's two children, Marina and Roman, were evidently more personable. The Princess caught Pridham's eye: 'a tall, good-looking girl of 27, very jolly, I should think, at times

Grand Duchess Anastasia, the younger of the 'Black Peril'

unlike the present'. Marina does, indeed, smile in most of the photographs from the *Marlborough*; she had generous features in a small, oval face.

And, although he was less striking than his sister, 22-year-old Roman would soon become a familiar figure on deck, befriending the officers over cigarettes. The Prince's

Militsa's jolly daughter, Marina, who caught Pridham's eye

service on the Turkish front as a second lieutenant in a Caucasian Sappers Regiment had done little to alter the slim and ascetic appearance he had inherited from his father. Thin lips and hooded eyes, a further paternal legacy, tended to lend him a slightly supercilious expression. But the tone of his memoir, 'At The Court of the Last Tsar', is unfailingly generous. Pridham noted the Prince as 'a delicate young man'. The Prince, in his turn, declared himself taken, from the start, by 'the friendly Pridham'.

The young Prince had actually been the last of his immediate family to arrive at the jetty, as he had run to the top of a favourite hill for a last view of the Black Sea. He later recounted how he sat on his accustomed rock clutching a small case containing what he referred to as all his worldly possessions. As he sat, his free hand had fallen upon an axe in a crevice: succumbing to a superstitious urge, he had put the axe in his case and vowed to keep it close by him forever.

After assembling on deck, the Dulbers set about laying claim to cabins. None of the British officers spoke Russian and Princess Marina was the only one of the party who spoke good English. But a first glance at the fearsome Grand Duke Nicholas was probably enough to persuade the officers that his entourage was entitled to the best accommodation.

Pridham, who should have been in charge of the allocation of the cabins, was, at this crucial moment, in some confusion. As he scrutinised the growing number of passengers, he struggled to match faces with the names on his list. After the Dulbers it was, curiously, the quietly dressed Youssoupov whose appearance he found particularly intriguing. The officer noted the 32-year-old Youssoupov's subtler charms with satisfaction: 'Prince Youssoupov (Jun)' – to distinguish Felix from his father – 'educated at Oxford, thoroughly English looking and speaks it well.'

Clearly Youssoupov's aim was now to project himself as the stiff and proper Edwardian gentleman *comme il faut*. Among his more obscure skills was an aptitude for tennis: in 1913 the Tsar declared him, in his diary, the best player in Russia. The Prince had thoroughly enjoyed his days at Oxford, cultivating extreme eccentricities, including breeding hens in his room and distributing alms to the poor. This last task he performed in a white suit, throwing sovereigns from a balcony and savouring ensuing scuffles on the pavement.

As the murderer of the 'holy man' who had scandalised the society of St Petersburg with his passion for 'driving out sin with sin', Youssoupov had been feted, and once even mooted as a potential ruler of Russia. He himself recalled with pride the words of the leader of the Russian Parliament, the Duma: 'The Duma leader rose as I came in: "Moscow wishes to proclaim you Emperor. What do you say?"'

Soon after the murder, in December 1916, Felix had witnessed crowds gathering to pray outside his palace. Four months after the Revolution, he was proudly dining in the fateful cellar, displaying a blood-stained polar bear rug to his distinguished English visitor, Emmeline Pankhurst.

Since arriving in the Crimea, he had enjoyed a further empowering meeting with an elderly nun in Yalta. He later claimed the nun smelt of flowers, despite having lived in a window-less cell for nine years. She had greeted him exuberantly: 'You've come – I've been expecting you as the saviour of our country... Rasputin was a fiend whom you destroyed as St George slew the dragon... You will take an active part in the restoration of Russia. Remember he who opened the door must be the one to close it.'

Curiously, Grand Duke Nicholas, perhaps at the behest of his wife, also visited an elderly mystic in Yalta. This mystic, possibly the same one, told the Grand Duke she'd had a vision that he, too, was Russia's saviour.

Within the last few months, a German emissary had asked Youssoupov to be Tsar so he could legitimise the Brest-

Litovsk peace agreement. He had, of course, dutifully turned down the offer.

As he collected himself on deck, Youssoupov may have relished the idea of confounding expectation. He would have liked to imagine the sailors struggling to link this demure gentleman with the brutal killing of Rasputin. In his memoir he savours every moment of the murder, detailing the trapping, poisoning, shooting and finally grappling: 'It seemed that the devil himself, incarnate in this muzhik, was holding me in vice-like fingers, never to let me go.' His description includes the haunting detail that Rasputin kept repeating his name 'Felix'. In fact, over the preceding few months, the pair had seen so much of each other that Rasputin had his own oddly affectionate name for Youssoupov: 'the little one'.

According to one report, a mysterious Englishman had come to say goodbye to Youssoupov on the quay: an Oxford friend, the British spy Oswald Rayner. It is now believed that Rayner was at Youssoupov's palace on the night of the killing. It is even rumoured that it was Rayner's bullet which finally dispatched 'Dark Forces': the British secret service's code name for Rasputin. Such was Rayner's enduring attachment to Youssoupov that, years later, he named his son John Felix Rayner after him.

Members of the British community were certainly on hand at the time of the murder. It was the British chaplain, Bishop Reverend Lombard, who had finally cleansed the bloody cellar with holy water and incense. The night after the killing, it was Lady Sybil Grey who protected Youssoupov from Rasputin's supporters by admitting him to the English hospital with a fishbone stuck in his throat. Within a few weeks of the murder, the British Foreign Office was receiving what Duff Cooper, who had known Felix in Oxford, referred to as 'thrilling telegrams' about the affair.

Youssoupov was a mythmaker and his bizarre reputation would have gone before him even among the lowlier members of the English crew. Some of these may have been further thrown by his apparent lack of effeminacy. When he

Felix Youssoupov, now apparently reformed of his former effeminate streak, and indeed accompanied by an arrestingly pretty young wife, Princess Irina, a niece of the Tsar

was born, his formidable mother, already having one son, refused to let her fervent desire for a daughter be thwarted: she raised her pretty second child as a girl. In common with Lady Speranza Wilde, who dressed her second son, Oscar, as a girl, the Princess kept the young Felix out of boy's clothes for longer than was wise. Cross-dressing became a habit and, as a teenager, Youssoupov became known on the St Petersburg social circuit as a woman. 'My mother's caprice had a lasting effect on my character,' as he put it laconically. King Edward VII himself took a shine to the boy: 'Tell me, who is that lovely young woman?' he once asked Youssoupov's brother.

There had formerly been an effeminate streak even in his espousal of monarchist principles. As an adolescent, he had kept fresh flowers under portraits of Louis XVI and Marie Antoinette.

Now, however, Youssoupov was apparently reformed and indeed accompanied by an arrestingly pretty, fragile-looking young wife. Princess Irina, aged 24, whom he had married five years before, was the niece of the Tsar and a classic beauty with wide-set eyes and clearly defined high cheekbones. Pridham continues in his diary: 'His wife Princess Irina is the elder child of Gr Duchess Xenia, very small and shy and looks much too frail to have such a healthy child as the baby Irina is, now aged about five.'

In fact, during the early months of the family's captivity in the Crimea, Princess Irina had shown her mettle by travelling to St Petersburg to beg the Provisional Leader, Kerensky, for better treatment, particularly for her grandmother, the Dowager. But Princess Irina's bravery was not matched by worldliness. It was said that as she was being courted by Youssoupov, she did not know the meaning of the word 'homosexual'.

At the news of their impending departure from the Crimea, Irina had made the curious decision to rush, first, to collect copies of the family's samizdat newspaper, the *Merry Arnold*, on which she had worked. Her energy in this direction was unlikely to have been fuelled by worries about political content, as the newspaper mainly featured travel articles about trips to imaginary lands. But, by the 13th edition, she had clearly developed a strong sentimental attachment to the enterprise. The 14th edition foundered when all the staff were laid low with Spanish flu. Latterly the *Merry Arnold* had become a sort of cause in itself, with editorial meetings opening and closing with a hymn.

Pridham noted the contrast between the conventionally dressed young couple and Youssoupov's warrior-like father. As he wrote of the elder Prince, once Governor of Moscow: 'Another person of outstanding appearance, also wearing Cossack costume.'

Before the Revolution, one estimate of the Youssoupovs' estate placed the value of their possessions at between 300 and 350 million dollars. The couple held parties for 2,000 guests at their Fontanka Palace; the elder Prince Felix once presented his wife with a mountain for her birthday. They had estates in 17 provinces which they visited in style, on a private train complete with an aviary.

Within a few days of the Youssoupovs' boarding, Pridham seems to have been told not only that 'Youssoupov (sen)', as he called him, was 'perhaps the greatest landowner in Russia', but also that he mismanaged his estates. As the Youssoupovs' affairs were not well known outside Russia, Pridham's information must have come from an ill-wisher on board: 'He owned enormous estates in various parts of the country, in these and the immediate vicinity there was no poverty, but a very great deal was wasted in unnecessary charity. With better organisation, the wealth could have been distributed further afield.'

The Prince had shone no better in office. He had been

Youssoupov père, whose warrior-like appearance,
as Pridham noted, was in complete contrast to his
conventionally dressed son

dismissed from his job in 1915 because of his mishandling
of anti-German riots. He had allowed the looters and ri-
oters a free hand and then, only at a late stage, sent in the
police. Such was the police's subsequent ineptitude that they
bricked up German wine shops with looters and revellers
still lying unconscious inside.

Known as a rough, even brutal military man, the elder
Prince Felix was heavily moustached, later refusing to shave
even when Stalin rose to power championing the same look.
His wife, Princess Zenaide, complained, in 1922, to one of the
Tsar's nephews: 'It's really awful to think Stalin looks exactly
like my husband.'

Meanwhile, the formidable Princess, once so determined to

have a daughter, had been a great beauty and had been painted by Serov in 1902. She had established herself as an actress of some standing and had at one point even been approached by Stanislavsky. In the end, she had eschewed the stage, preferring to declaim in person. Years before the Revolution, she found herself banned from the Court for unashamedly airing her disapproval of Rasputin. Relations had not improved with her husband's dismissal.

As the embarkation progressed, the sailors grew innured to the unusual sight of women emerging on deck; so innured, indeed, that that the arrival of the last two went entirely unnoticed. Pridham later described in his memoir how he suddenly spotted 'two unaccompanied ladies evidently uncertain as to where they should go. I was about to ask them who they were when I suddenly realised that one of them, an elderly little lady dressed in black, closely resembled our Queen Alexandra, and could be none other than the Dowager Empress Marie herself. At this moment Count Pavel Fersen (one of Grand Duke Nicholas' retinue) came forward and, after saluting the Empress, presented me to her and to the Grand Duchess Xenia who accompanied her.'

In the diary he kept on board Pridham tells the story slightly differently: 'I found I had been speaking to her (Xenia) and the Empress for some time before I rumbled who even the latter was, and much longer before I knew that my 'first lieutenant' was the Tsar's own sister.'

The mortified First Lieutenant subsequently gave vent to the fury he felt at the time. 'I learned later to my disgust that the officer of the watch, who had strict injunctions from me to ensure that I should be at the head of the gangway when the Empress Marie arrived alongside, had lost his head and omitted to let anyone know that she had arrived, or to accompany

Above, the Dowager
Empress Marie; and
right, her daughter the
Grand Duchess Xenia
– both of whom 'used a
bold gaze and upright
posture to offset
diminutive frames'

her to the Captain's quarters. His excuse was that boats were
arriving alongside in quick succession at both sides of the
ship at the same time. I never learned what the Captain and
Commander thought about this terrible lapse.'

In fact, had he broached the subject with either officer,
he would have discovered that their feeling was simply overwhelming relief that the Dowager was finally on board. Both
would have been all too aware of the unstinting attempts that
had been made to persuade her to leave the Crimea. King
Victor Emanuel III of Italy, whose consort was a sister of the
Black Peril, had tried to entice all the Romanovs to Italy. King
Nicholas of Montenegro had issued an invitation; the King
of Roumania had sent a Canadian envoy. But as she told the
English Commander Turle 'nothing would induce her to go
to Roumania in that little ship'. Meanwhile, the biggest success Turle's envoy had enjoyed was gratifying the Dowager's
yearning for white bread: 'Fancy me being asked for bread by
an Empress!'

Her final capitulation to Captain Johnson was of course
only brought by his agreement to organise the rescue of her
fellow refugees; the *Marlborough*, she stipulated, must be the
last of the rescue ships to leave Russia. The Captain met her
conditions mostly with good grace.

The lapse of protocol regarding the Dowager may have
sharpened Pridham's senses as he recorded his first impressions of the Ai-Todors. In any case, he was full of admiration,
particularly noting Grand Duchess Xenia's youthful vigour:
'one of the youngest looking grandmothers I have ever seen.'
Xenia had been celebrating her 44th birthday when Captain
Johnson had first announced his visit. She was small and neat-
looking with a clearly defined forehead and cheekbones and a
generous, resolute mouth. Her large eyes, set wide apart, were

inclined to an unshrinking gaze, She had wasted no time in gathering together jewellery and a 54-piece set of solid gold plate.

She was now accompanied by five of her six sons, ranging

Xenia's five dashing sons. Young Vassily is on the right

in age from 11 to 21, all of them dark and handsome in their different ways and all of whom found equal favour with Pridham as 'cheerful youngsters'. As Pridham tried to register them all, it was the fourth son, Dmitri, aged 18, who struck him particularly as 'looking exactly like an English public school boy'.

Prince Dmitri remembered all the brothers being warned early of their impending departure and starting to pack immediately. They had been dismayed to be told that they were to be limited to one trunk and two small suitcases each. After much agonising, Dmitri settled on some curious choices to take into exile: pieces of old Russian china and several books, including a rare volume on the Imperial Porcelain factory at St Petersburg. More poignant were the bags that the boys filled with soil from the part of their estate – Ai-Todor – most dear to them: 'My piece came from near the little house which I used for my cookery,' recalled Dmitri, who had, since early boyhood, been a keen chef.

While noting the Dowager's resemblance to Queen Alexandra, Pridham was struck afresh by the resemblance between the Dowager and Xenia. Mother and daughter shared clearly defined facial features, though the Dowager's were softened by her eyes: smaller and less Slavic-looking than Xenia's. Both used a bold gaze and posture to offset diminutive frames.

But no amount of boldness could have masked the Dowager's current unease. She had barely recovered from the flurry of packing. According to her youngest grandson, Vassily, she had refused to contemplate preparing for a life in exile. He later insisted that she had considered herself as facing no more than an extended trip. Adamant that her domestic staff should not be obliged to beg for immediate necessities, she had packed only cookware, kitchen utensils and linen.

She had, however, been sufficiently concerned about the future to bring along her two Pekingese, Chi Foo and Soon. Chi Foo had already earned his moment in history when the doughty Dowager held him up in derision for his name to be recorded during a Bolshevik roll-call. As Prince Dmitri recalled: 'she became red in the face, as she did when cross and shouted down to the intruders: "and don't forget the dog!"'

As Pridham accompanied her and Xenia to the Captain's cabin, he was obliged to address most of what he said to

Xenia, since her English was better than her mother's. He was full of his own difficulties, admitting that he was unclear as to how many people were embarking or who they were. But, as the party progressed down the ship's corridors, he sensed that the women were exercised by some issue beyond either the sorrow of departure or the immediate confusion. By the time the small party reached the Captain's cabin, he had learnt from Xenia that things were far from straightforward between her mother and the Grand Duke Nicholas. Only later would he discover the full extent of the bad blood between these two principal members of the Romanov party.

The problem currently at issue was sadly prosaic: Grand Duke Nicholas's adjutant, Count Pavel Fersen, had earmarked the best cabins for the Dulbers. The Dowager, who should have had first choice, was incandescent: 'I greeted all the officers and went down. There we found a huge disorder; the Dulbers had taken all the best cabins for themselves and theirs so that Xenia and all the Ai-Todors could only have what was left over. Incredibly impertinent... I have never known anything of the like.'

She was further annoyed not to be able to address her complaints to Nikolasha himself. The Grand Duke had been taken off alone by one of the officers immedately after his arrival on board. And none of the sailors could shed any light on the arrangements: 'When I asked the good gentlemen who had given orders, they naturally did not know anything.'

However, she then fully acknowledged Pridham's efforts as he stepped adroitly into the turbulent water, hastily agreeing to reorganise the accommodation with Xenia. 'There was a charming officer Pridham who suggested to Xenia that he would arrange everything as best possible together with her.' She declared herself satisfied with 'the Captain's lovely cabin and beautiful drawingroom'.

Pridham, in turn, happily immersed himself in what was finally a clear brief: 'From then on it was plain sailing. Count Fersen faded away, I think with a flea in his ear... and I found myself closeted with an extremely charming and capable woman who knew exactly what was entailed and had very clear ideas as to how details should be settled, and that, most certainly, they would be so settled, whatever Count Fersen may have schemed.'

His wide-eyed admiration for Xenia was reciprocated. She fondly nicknamed him 'Job' in recognition of his travails. 'So our first list was quickly torn up and the job done in half an hour, including the impossible one for me, of giving the necessary orders to the Russian servants now beginning to arrive on board.' He embellished the details in his diary. 'She (Xenia) being able to speak fluent English and being obviously worth half a dozen of their men is more help to me than all the remainder put together.'

He was further impressed when Xenia refused the cabin he had allotted her next to the Captain's cabin, insisting on taking a small, dark, windowless compartment below deck. She thoughtfully opted for a so-called 'potted-air' cabin, behind the ship's side-armour, in order that her mother's maid, Kiki, could sleep next to her mistress.

Prince Dmitri and his two younger brothers slept in hammocks in the ship's schoolroom. As he said: 'Although we were later offered a more conventional resting place I continued using the hammock as I found it extremely comfortable.' The youngest brother, Vassily, also recalled the hammocks being popular; though some were clearly more popular than others, as there were arguments over who was going to sleep in which. Pridham distributed mattresses for the five young children under six: 'the matter had become urgent.. the mothers declared with my entire sympathy... the poor mites being fretful in strange surroundings.'

Pridham then witnessed further generosity of spirit, this time from one of the Dulbers – Princess Marina, whose jolly looks had already caught his eye. He would have been particularly struck as it was so obviously a kindness *'de haut en bas'*, from a mistress to a servant.

Princess Marina had been assigned a small cabin with a single berth; a second mattress had been put on the floor for her maid. But because the elderly maid suffered from a bad back, Marina had insisted she take the berth as well as the extra mattress from the floor. As he wrote in his diary: 'I found that she had given up her bunk to her maid who is rather shaky and was preparing to sleep on the deck on a blanket only, I had taken the precaution to keep one or two mattresses up my sleeve so was able to make a slightly better arrangement for that night in spite of her protestation to the effect that she was used to it, having been a Red Cross nurse for two years in the fighting in the Caucasus.'

It was Marina who later helped Pridham sort out piles of cases and other bits of luggage left on deck with no names. The luggage arrived after the passengers and, apart from the Dowager's monogram on several small suitcases, was completely unlabelled. As Pridham said in his memoir: 'had it not been for Princess Marina... offering to help as an interpreter, most of the rest of the luggage would have become hopelessly mixed up'. Her younger brother, Prince Roman, made no bones about Marina's contribution, describing her as 'a redeeming angel'. However, he also paid tribute, once more, to Pridham: 'we became friendly with this sympathetic officer.'

Pridham later reflected wryly upon the kindness of

members of the Imperial Family towards their servants: 'Yet these were the people who had for years been accused of being pitiless tyrants, holding their people in bonds of cruel slavery. In those days we had not yet learned to suspect or recognise the insidiousness of Leftist propaganda.'

Having settled the Romanovs, Pridham still faced the vexed question of accommodating the various remaining servants. He appeared to find this altogether more difficult, though it may have been that their masters and mistresses had simply exhausted his goodwill. He may, alternatively, have been prejudiced against them, believing them tarred with the same brush as their rabble-rousing revolutionary brothers and sisters. 'The Russian maids and manservants are much more nuisance. The latter I have gathered into the Wardroom bathroom flat, the former are more difficult to deal with.'

Years later, Pridham tempered his criticisms: 'The latter (the servants) spoke no English and only rarely a little French and being obviously dazed by their sudden upheaval and unusual surroundings they struck me at first as being rather indolent.'

In the early days of 1917, the servants at Ai-Todor had appeared to revel in the idea of the Revolution as a sort of fiesta. They had carried on serving their masters in full livery with red ribbons fluttering from their buttonholes; some even sewed pieces of red material over the Imperial Eagle on their gilt buttons. The idea was that the ribbons and bits of material would be untied and unpicked when, as Prince Dmitri put it, things returned to normal. With these happy gestures the servants had acknowledged the larger upheavals.

But as it became clear that things would never return to normal, the servants' position had grown more precarious by the day. The attitude of the new regime towards 'slaves of former masters' was not sympathetic. Any former landowner brave enough to request concessions for their starving dependents faced an outcry from the peasants: 'serves them right... let them fend for themselves now.'

Aboard the *Marlborough*, the servants gave every indication that they had run out of gestures. If their masters were in dire straits, where did that leave them? Unsure of their roles as servants, less sure of their roles as workers and rebels, they now waited passively, obliged to deal with whatever destiny threw their way.

~~~~~

Late in the evening of that first night, dinner was served in the Captain's drawing room for all the grandees: the Dowager, Grand Duchess Xenia, Grand Duke Nicholas, Grand Duke Peter and the Black Peril. The Dowager was not pleased; she clearly felt that she and her immediate family should have been served separately. But she could not bring herself to express the exact source of her displeasure in her diary: 'We all dined together, the two brothers with their black wives, their children. It was all heartbreaking, but at the same time outrageous.'

Pridham very nearly found himself part of this awkward dinner. He was invited to join the party by the Dowager and did not know how to answer. Fortunately, his helpmate, Grand Duchess Xenia, explained that he would be much too busy; thus, he said, he avoided an 'outrageous betise'.

The Captain did end up dining with the Romanovs, seated next to Felix's mother, the former beauty, Princess Zenaide Youssoupov. He was unlikely to have been ruffled by tricky undercurrents. In any case, as it turned out, with all the

Dowager's reservations, this first dinner went relatively smoothly, several diners even remaining at the table after eating. Prince Roman, however, was glad to take refuge in the cabin he shared with his father. He made no complaints about his lowly mattress on the floor.

As Pridham continued his duties on deck, he came across Miss 'Nana' Coster, the Grand Duchess Xenia's English nanny. He quickly formed a good opinion of her. As an Englishwoman with integrity at the centre of this unexpectedly thorny court, her perspective would have been invaluable.

Miss Coster's credentials were impeccable: her sister had acted as a nanny to the Tsar's two elder daughters. Pridham was particularly impressed by her loyalty to the Dowager: 'There was no snobbery about it, she just worshipped the old lady and her heart was full with the appalling tragedy which had befallen them.'

The good-hearted Miss Coster was an independent thinker, managing to combine her more conventional passion for Pears and Cuticura soap with a firm belief in homeopathy. She invariably travelled, according to Prince Dmitri, with a chest from England containing alternative medicines, and she invented a flannel mat held by metal piping which took the chill off the children's marble tub.

Though she was strict with her charges, continually threatening to 'get the Japs' on to them, she was much loved. Their parents were equally attached to her, at one point giving her a fig tree of her own at Ai-Todor. The children were obliged to make a special request if they wanted any of its fruit.

And she was nothing if not versatile. She staged grand tableaux: 'my parents and staff watched as the curtains of an impromptu stage were drawn to reveal Irina, Theodor, Nikita, Rostislav and myself dressed as flowers', recalled

Prince Dmitri. 'I was a rose all in pink, Rostislav was a poppy and the rest were other flowers. We sat motionless on the stage while everyone clapped.' But she had also willingly set her hand to less appealing tasks. It was Miss Coster who was in charge of an unsavoury 'pot' which would be fished out of a leather case while the children were travelling in a closed landau: 'the contents would be emptied out of the window at an appropriate moment by Nana'.

Through all the turbulent months in the Crimea, Miss Coster had continued with the Princes' English lessons. As Dmitri wrote to his English tutor Mr Herbert Stewart: 'All the revolution we had lessons with Papa and Mr Urgenson and English with Miss Coster... Our dictations in English are very nice and reading too I try my best to imporoove. I read all the book which I find only English.' His younger brother, Vassily, remembered studying the misleadingly titled *Reading Without Tears* with Miss Coster. 'That generally ended up with both of us crying – I from despair and Nana from exasperation.'

Efforts had been made to create a normal life for the children. That first spring, in 1917, had been largely a curiously halcyon period, though there were flies in the ointment: Xenia was exercised against the notion of workers' rights. She wrote: 'In Koreiz they brought in a new hideous eight-hour working day and are demanding that in all estates everybody including house servants must not work more than that!'

Xenia's main preoccupation at Ai-Todor had been her rose garden; her youngest son, Vassily, would pick off dead roses and seed pods while she collected the day's roses. The other brothers, meanwhile, would row on the lake and fish, or ride in the park, where moose and bison wandered loose. Dmitri remembered collecting pebbles on the beach, and dipping them in candle wax to make them shine.

In the opposing camp, at Dulber, Militsa had been in deep discussion with the gardener as they planned new plants for autumn and the following spring. Her son, Prince Roman, spent time sharing cigarettes and chatting desultorily with the guards; topics included politics, philosophy and, most popularly, his family.

There was even a wedding, with Roman and Marina's sister, Princess Nadezhda, marrying Prince Nicholas Orloff. Xenia took time off from her rose garden to watch the ceremony. As she wrote: 'This afternoon Mama and all of us went to Xarax and watched Nadia and N. Orloff's wedding from afar... Nikolasha and Petiusha (Grand Dukes Nicholas and Peter) were also in Circassian coats. Serge Leucht in civvies with a red tie. We couldn't see the bride properly but Marina was in a fantastic nurses' dress.'

At this point the Dowager appeared to be bearing up well. She attended the funeral of the young wife of her equerry, Serge Dolgorouky, at Koreiz. An Englishman, Bertie Stopford, who had made the journey from St Petersburg to the Crimea to attend, was impressed: 'Empress looking better than I expected,' he recorded cheerfully in his diary. He added, however, that the service had had to be abandoned because of the rain.

But she was not to be altogether consoled by a low-key funeral, still less by the rose gardens. She wrote to her brother Waldemar: 'Everything is awful beyond description and I only wonder that I am still alive... We live a very quiet existence, walk a great deal in the lovely garden, where everything is flowering so magnificently. But one cannot enjoy anything when one is so unhappy and profoundly sad and disconsolate.'

Her tone during these early days in the Crimea was frequently more petulant than fearful. She was, for some while, unable to grasp the danger of her position. The British Ambassador in St Petersburg, Sir George Buchanan, wrote a personal memo to England following a visit from Youssoupov. Youssoupov had brought letters from the Dowager to be sent to England: 'I also pointed out that the Empress was running a great risk in sending the letters by private persons for transmission, as if it was discovered it would compromise both Her Majesty and myself. Prince said he entirely agreed but that unfortunately Empress and other members of the Imperial Family entirely failed to appreciate their position.'

And what of the Tsar? It was during Pridham's first chat on deck with Miss Coster that he learnt about the Dowager's refusal to believe reports about the murders of her son, the Tsar, and his family. He wrote in his diary: 'The Imperial Family are apparently still uncertain about the death of the Tsar and his children.'

After the murders, in July 1918, memorial services had been held in the chapel at Xenia's estate, Ai-Todor. The Dowager, in denial about the deaths, had refused to attend. Grand Dukes Nicholas and Peter and their families had also stayed away out of respect for her. With all her reservations about the Dulbers, she had been grateful for their support: she steeled herself to ask Militsa's son, Prince Roman, to pass on her thanks.

During the months leading up to her final departure, the Dowager's muddled state of grief and wishful thinking had made her susceptible to curious happenings. At one point she had been visited by a mysterious gypsy who appeared on a balcony at the estate where she was then staying proclaiming: 'Your son is healthy and feels well.' The bearer of such happy news was rewarded with 25 roubles. In reply to a letter of condolence from King Christian of Denmark, the Dowager had written a crisp response: 'After several weeks of terrifying suspense and proclamations, I have been assured that he and his family have been released and brought to a place of safety...'

However, she had remained plagued by uncertainties and in September 1918, two months after the murders, she wrote to her sister Alix: 'Since I was assured that poor, beloved Nicky had been set free & taken to safety, I have heard no more, so you can imagine how terrible this ignorance torments me night & day. It is a good thing that they keep secret where he & the family are, but I still find that they ought to send someone to me who could tell me he really is safe, just to settle me. You can become completely mad with fear & worry in the end. I am simply amazed that I am still living with this épée de Damocles hanging over my head...'

Pridham later thought that Xenia and the Dowager were unaware, during their journey on the *Marlborough*, that the stories of the deaths had been published in *The Times*. As he said years later: 'Thinking about it now, I think it was quite surprising, as it was in *The Times*, you say in July 1918, yes. I didn't know that. A person who I did see so much many years afterwards was the Grand Duchess Xenia... I know for certain that she never knew it until much later.'

Asked in the same interview how often he had seen the Dowager in the course of the voyage, and whether he was in a position to judge her state of mind, Pridham confirmed that he had seen the Dowager two or three times a day, every day. 'I once saw her laugh, at dinner one night... we'd been on board about a week. She did smile happily at somebody's remark around the dinner table.'

In fact, even British spies in Russia remained uncertain about what had happened to the Imperial Family for several months after *The Times* articles appeared. Sir Robert Bruce Lockhart had been sent by Lloyd George to head a mission to establish unofficial relations with the Bolsheviks. As late as February 9th, 1919, he wrote in his diary: 'It now appears that both the Tsar and Tsarina and all children have been murdered, also the Grand Duchess Elizabeth and probably the Grand Duke Michael.'

Years later, one of the *Marlborough* sailors, WG 'Robbie' Roberts, who had observed members of the Imperial Family closely during religious services, gave his testimony to the Imperial War Museum: 'One thing I do know is that neither the Dowager Empress nor members of her family on board believed the Tsar and his family were murdered.'

The news may have been of such a magnitude that it could not be fully accepted. According to Youssoupov, there were rumours circulating in the Crimea that the Tsar and his family had been shot, but nobody believed them. The stories would frequently be denied in newspaper reports. Youssoupov remembered reading a letter written by an officer who insisted he had saved the Imperial Family.

But Prince Dmitri later wrote that his family had been told about the murders when the Allies first arrived in the Crimea after the Armistice. His account indicates that Xenia and her family had been told the news and believed it to be true. This would obviously run counter to Pridham's impression on the *Marlborough*.

That first night, Pridham speculated long and hard about the Russian psyche. Previously he had met yet another colourful member of the Imperial Family, Grand Duke Boris. In the course of the previous few weeks, Boris and two lady friends had visited several of the British battleships in a bid to get a passage to Constantinople. Asking for permission to travel on the *Marlborough*, he had told Pridham he did not want to travel on a French ship as he disliked the French. Unknown to Pridham, Boris also had a reputation for disliking the English.

Pridham had replied that the Dowager would have to decide whether the trio could travel with the rest of the Romanovs. But she clearly turned them down; after they were dispatched from the ship, Pridham never saw them again. It is not clear whether it had been Grand Duke Boris the Dowager objected to or the ladies: a mother and her young daughter who, Pridham noted, was a 'startlingly pretty lady'. Boris had told Pridham he was penniless, with just 12 roubles to his name: 'he wore a very old suit and his hat looked as if he had picked it up in the street.'

The Captain of one of the other battleships that Boris petitioned, HMS *Calypso*, described him in a letter to the BBC in 1971: 'a rather bloated looking man in an old bicycling suit and dusty brogues.' Captain MF Wilson, of Worthington, reported with glee how Boris had asked one of the ship's engineers how the King was: 'Oh very well,' the engineer replied.

On the HMS *Calypso*, Boris had apparently drunk whisky from teatime until midnight and within the next two days had fled from Yalta, abandoning his faithful adjutant without a penny: 'We do not think highly of this Grand Duke,' concluded Wilson. Boris and the two ladies eventually managed to escape, settling in France, where he lived until his death in 1943.

The *Marlborough* officers had heard nothing of these damaging stories. In his diary, Pridham simply reported, in wonder, Boris's descriptions of his conflicted Cossacks:

'Grand Duke Boris told us that his own Cossacks, simple kind-hearted creatures, one day were risking their lives to recover the bodies of their officers killed by the Bolsheviks, and the next had suddenly and for no apparent reason turned completely round and were murdering their own officers with all the rest.'

Pridham added that, from what he heard, the White Army officers themselves were in an equally desperate, though less indecisive mood: 'at present their attitude here seems to be that they may just as well die for the forlorn hope of saving their country from the present regime, as live as exiles in foreign countries.'

In his memoir, Youssoupov offers particularly graphic descriptions of the suffering of White officers during the Bolshevik uprisings in Yalta. He expanded upon Captain Johnson's tales of the Black Sea Fleet flinging their officers overboard with weights on their feet: 'a diver sent down to explore the bottom of the bay went mad at the sight of corpses standing upright, swaying in currents.'

Youssoupov claimed he saw Bolshevik sailors openly displaying booty stolen from Russian aristocrats. In a description that sounds like a sexual fantasy, he talked of sailors powdered and made up, with necklaces on their hairy chests. As if to reassure the reader, he sums it up as a 'masquerade in hell'.

As the passengers started going to bed, Captain Johnson ordered the *Marlborough* to weigh anchor. Roman gazed with emotion at the changing coastline as the ship travelled the hour to Yalta. Through the gathering darkness he was able to make out his father's estate, Dulber, then Tchair, Xarax, Ai-Todor and the Tsar's palace, Livadia. When he went to his cabin he found it empty; his father, the Grand Duke Peter, was, unexpectedly, up talking to the Dowager. What the couple found to talk about cannot be known: presumably not the accommodation debacle.

After night fell and the ship drew into Yalta, the steward Charles Henry Wakeling took a photograph to send back to his wife. 'This is a view of Yalta taken from the ship. Not very good but I thought I would like to have one as a memento of the occasion. Hope you are all well. We are quite fit. You should get a letter by this same mail. Nice weather here but very hot.' Not much is known about Charles Wakeling beyond his sense of historic and aesthetic moment. His Naval record testified to his complexion being 'fresh' and 'sallow'. His stated occupation, as carpenter, was borne out by his long weeks at sea spent carving an 18-foot three-dimensional puzzle of a brick tower.

At Yalta that night the *Marlborough* received a naval signal from another battleship, the *Northesk*: 'Will evacuate 1500 Russian subjects to Novorissisk and 400 to Sevastapol tomorrow Tuesday. I will get Allied subjects on board *Northesk*. Request *Montrose* may call here for them on her way back to Sevastopol.'

A photograph of Yalta, at night, taken by the steward
Charles Wakeling, to send back to his wife

Day 2

Roman was woken early by a loud rattling at his door as a sailor polished the cabin doorknob. In some embarrassment, he dressed quickly and walked to the deck. Smoke poured from the ships' funnels. Clouds shrouded the mountains behind the town. He was impressed as he watched the sailors cleaning the ship, repairing damaged paint work and scrubbing the deck.

In fact, Pridham was suffering agonies over the state of the ship. 'To our chagrin, the ship was far below an acceptable standard in smartness: just out from England and dockyard hands and having been under steam since we left three weeks ago, we sorely needed an uninterrupted spell of "clean ship" routine before we could render our coal-burning battleship fit for the duty she was being called upon to perform.'

As Roman walked on deck, the officers would specially stop work in order to exchange pleasantries. In the course of the next few days, he would be taken on several tours of the ship; after these he would drink whisky in the officers' mess.

The officers' generosity with their cigarettes would have been particularly appreciated. Most of the Romanov party were avid smokers, with the Dowager at the helm. She had begun chain-smoking primarily, it was said, to annoy her daughter-in-law, the Tsarina. But if she had been keen for her habit to be noted by the Tsarina, she was as keen to hide it from others. As Prince Dmitri recalled: 'She often smoked in private but did not like the servants to see her and if one entered the room when she was smoking, she would hide the cigarette behind her back, oblivious of the smoke rising above her shoulders.' When Commander Turle had visited her earlier in the year, he had brought her cigarettes with the newspapers.

Cigarettes had been a source of comfort for the party during the unsettling years in the Crimea. However, at one point, after a dinner party at the Youssoupovs' 'Eagle's Nest' house, Youssoupov had handed out cigarettes which exploded when lit. A lesser joker would have been dismayed by the guests' reaction: terrified that they were under attack, they ran from the house. For Youssoupov, his guests' terror was the icing on the cake.

Meanwhile, on the *Marlborough*, the officers' readiness with their packets belied strict regulations regarding smoking. Any sailor below the age of 18 who was caught smoking would be confined to a cell for two or three days on what was referred to as 'low diet' – ie bread and water.

Upon his return to the cabin, Roman was pleasantly surprised with a further friendly gesture. A sailor who had brought his father morning tea had taken away Roman's hat and replaced its tattered band with a new one labelled 'HMS *Marlborough*'. The procedure had been carried out with so little ostentation that his father, in the cabin at the time, hadn't noticed. Roman confessed himself overwhelmed.

The thoughtfulness of the sailors was noticed and appreciated by all members of the party. The Tsarina's lady-in-waiting Countess Mengden's experiences in the Crimea were such that she had taken to sleeping with a knife under her pillow. She now paid tribute to the officers' generosity: 'All the officers had cleared their cabins and let us have them, while they themselves were content to sleep in the hold. When I lay in my bunk, I could see "my host's" family portraits all around me and many small keepsakes from his loved ones at home.

'Both officers and crew were very considerate towards us and seemed to understand the agonies our souls had experienced and especially had to suffer now as we were leaving our country.'

In recent years, the Romanovs and their entourages had not known what treatment to expect. The reverence to which they had been accustomed before the Revolution had given way at best to suspicion and at worst to murder.

When hostilities increased and the family was forced to move to Dulber, Grand Duke Nicholas and Anastasia had been obliged to walk from their estate between rows of armed sailors. At this point the fury and humiliation of both Grand Dukes was such that they had refused to move to a safer estate and hide in the wine cellar. They proudly declared that they would prefer to 'submit themselves to God'.

The only benign regime they had experienced had been presided over, confusingly, by Russia's war-time enemy, the

Germans. But even in this case, the Kaiser's aide-de-camp had made himself unpopular by arriving with an unattractive proposition: he would proclaim any Romanov tsar provided they countersign the humiliating Treaty of Brest-Litovsk, ceding a third of Russian territories to the Germans. They had all, of course, refused.

Such was the Germans' unpopularity that their orders had been to protect the Imperial Family but not address them, for fear of causing offence. The Germans found Nikolasha especially unfriendly. After Anastasia had so handily dispatched the general with her broom, her husband wrote a stiff letter to the German authorities saying that if they wanted to talk to him, they would have to take him as a prisoner of war.

The Dowager refused to have her room guarded by Germans, preferring her trusty Cossacks. 'Assistance from the enemies of Russia – never,' she spat. Prince Roman put it starkly: 'It was unbearable to contemplate that the War, which had cost such sacrifices, had ended so shamefully.'

Vladimir Nabokov captured the conflicted mood: 'Then one spring day in 1918 when the pink puffs of blossoming almond trees enlivened the dark mountainside, the Bolsheviks vanished and a singularly silent army of Germans replaced them. Patriotic Russians were torn between the animal relief of escaping native executioners and the necessity of owing their reprieve to a foreign invader – especially the Germans.'

The young Prince Dmitri, aged 17, wrote in faltering English to Mr Stewart: 'the only unhappines is to now that the germans are here...'. Then he seems to have heard, on a brighter note, that the Germans were being beaten: 'I am awfully glad that allies are beating the beasts... PS It is disgusting to see the germans every were.'

When the Germans tried to punish the Bolsheviks who

had been guarding the Romanovs, they found themselves facing opposition from the former captives themselves. After a period of prolonged stand-offs, it was Youssoupov who eventually broke the taboo, entering into talks with the beleaguered German Commander, who, he later wrote: 'was quite firmly convinced that their prolonged detention had driven the poor Grand Dukes mad'.

The Romanovs' Bolshevik Commandant had clearly won his captives over, despite being a revolutionary and notably ugly: according to the young Prince Dmitri, he looked like a gorilla. Xenia's husband, Sandro, said that he 'came to us a full fledged Bolshevik. Like many of his comrades, he believed that Lenin had come to establish a Paradise on earth. We, and his own common sense, opened his eyes'.

Once again, it had been Youssoupov who was most active in building bridges. Driven probably by no more than youthful impatience, he had welcomed the Bolshevik Commandant for secret talks, encouraging him to climb over his balcony on the ground floor. The loyalty of Grand Duke Nicholas and Grand Duke Peter, meanwhile, had been assured after the Commandant rescued their stepdaughter and daughter from Yalta, bringing both young women to the relative safety of Tchair.

The Germans, finding their friendly overtures continually rebuffed, bit back rather weakly, as Xenia recorded loftily in her diary: 'In Yalta they put out an announcement that anybody who speaks badly about the Germans will be deported from the Crimea. Stupid.'

After years as victims of these tribal vagaries, the Romanovs found the unfailing courtesy and kindness of the British sailors gratifying. Prince Roman, having just retrieved his newly mended hat from his cabin, now discovered that the *Marlborough* crew had even extended its welcome to the Romanovs' dogs.

As the English are traditionally seen as dog-lovers, perhaps Roman should have been less surprised to find provision made for 'unexpected four-legged passengers'. But he had, for some time, been worried about his dachshund, Mutzi, which was locked in his mother's cabin overnight. He was particularly exercised because he knew that Dowager and Xenia both had their dogs with them on deck.

Now he asked Grand Duchess Xenia's son, Prince Nikita, owner of Bobi, for advice. He was thrilled to hear that a corner had been set aside for dogs, complete with a box of sand for their 'needs'. In addition to Mutzi and Bobi, there were of course the Dowager's Chi Foo and Soon, and Xenia's Toby. Joining the canine party at Yalta would be a large hairy dog of indeterminate breed belonging to the Baroness Dolgorouky: Pupsik.

Upon arrival in England, all the dogs were to be quarantined. The Admiralty, clearly anticipating difficulties, sent a telegraph while the party was still en route: 'There will be no exceptions.'

❧

The Dowager was not in the same benevolent frame of mind as Prince Roman. Though she went on deck and conceded that the weather was beautiful, she had not enjoyed her first night on board. Her diary entry for April 8th begins: 'I didn't sleep well; there was such a noise and light in my cabin.' She had not forgotten the effrontery of Grand Duke Nicholas's party the previous night. 'We are many, too many on board, the people from Dulber, who got here first, established themselves everywhere and acted as if they were at home.'

The Dowager does not specify in what respect the Grand Ducal party had acted as though they were at home, but her dislike of impropriety was wide ranging. In 1911, she had complained to the director of the Imperial Theatre about an outfit of Nijinsky's which she deemed too revealing. Prince Dmitri retained a clear memory of the ensuing scandal: 'The director took my grandmother's complaint very seriously and Nijinsky was asked to leave the country.'

Now, beset with fatigue and malaise, the Dowager felt ill-prepared for her first sight of Yalta. The *Marlborough* was obliged to anchor at the port in order to pick up baggage and embark the last members of the Royal party: three Dolgoroukys, together with their nanny Miss King, as well as Grand Duke Peter's daughter Nadezhda and her husband and baby. The ship's crew was also charged with helping to oversee the general evacuation of White Russians, then still pouring into the sea port from all over the Empire.

The Dowager had not seen Yalta since the death of her husband, Tsar Alexander III, at Livadia 25 years before. He had been a bear of a man, whose party tricks included walking through doors without opening them and bending forks in knots, but the couple were devoted to each other. Just before he died, Alexander wrote a most moving letter to his sister-in-law, Queen Alexandra, in which he asked her to take care of his wife after his death. Alix took her commission seriously, even sleeping in her heartbroken sister's bedroom at Yalta.

'It was the first time I saw Yalta again which cannot be recognised, it has become such a big town,' wrote the Dowager as she surveyed the busy port. 'What gruesome, heartbreaking memories for me after the last time I left this beloved place after my boundless pain and irreplaceable loss of my blessed and above everything, beloved Sasha...

'Now it is also dreadfully difficult, but at the same time it is such a bitter feeling to leave the country like this because of the fault of evil-minded people!'

Xenia also wrote in her diary of her sorrow at leaving: '...to have to sever oneself from one's own people, to say nothing of the grief of departing from Ai-Todor – home, the motherland.'

Grand Duchess Xenia had been particularly attached to her Crimean estate. She had written to her sister, Olga, in 1915, insisting that she be buried at Ai-Todor rather than in the sepulchral church in the Peter and Paul Fortress at St Petersburg where the Romanovs were traditionally laid. 'I had lunch at Anitchkov & then went with Mama to the fortress, on Amama's (her maternal grandmother's) anniversary... Cheerless & I hate (que Dieu me pardonne!) the fortress – makes one feel miserable. Remember to bury me at Ai-Todor – under a cypress tree near our little church!'

The Dowager's reveries were brought to an end as she was reminded of Yalta's more pressing problems. According to Youssoupov, it was his wife, the deceptively timid-looking Irina, who initially reminded the Dowager of the desperate straits of Yalta's refugees. Much upset, the Dowager immediately sent for the Captain. He could not have been looking forward to a further encounter with the doughty Dowager; he would still have been smarting after their prickly exchange of the night before.

His worst fears were borne out as, after a cursory apology from the Dowager, he found himself facing a barrage of requests, then demands and finally threats. She told him that if he even thought of setting sail before the last ship had gone, she would disembark and travel with the rest of the refugees. His eventual retort, that he had orders to leave the next day, was batted away as she insisted that she would explain the situation to the Admiral herself. At this point, in exasperation, the Captain again gave way. In the end the ship was anchored off Yalta for three days.

The Dowager did not mind complaining or being abusive in her diary and it is hard to imagine the Captain conceding defeat with a good grace. But perhaps some native survival instinct prevented the Dowager from demonising this man on whom so much of her destiny depended, even in the privacy of her diary. Her report of their exchange is brief and buoyant. She wrote: 'I have offered an apology to Capt Johnson after which I hope we will be good friends. I also told him that I do not want to leave before everyone from Yalta and surroundings has been evacuated. He is excellent and has promised to do everything he can.'

The original plan had been for the Dolgoroukys (the elderly Baroness Olga, and her two granddaughters) to embark with the Romanovs at Koreiz, but there had been some confusion when the Baroness's estate manager went missing. The family had initially been installed on another ship, the *Grafton*. As the elder granddaughter Sofka recalled, 'It (HMS *Grafton*) was packed. Granny was allotted the Captain's Cabin, Miss King and I secured a corner on the floor of the Officers' Mess.'

She had been aware that their transfer to the *Marlborough* was a privilege and that the company was more select. But this had not made her any happier about leaving the Crimea. Sofka was then a strikingly pretty 11-year-old with an impish face and long plaits; her grandmother was small, stocky and Slavic-looking with a round face, close-set hooded eyes and a disdainful expression.

Sofka had been told to prepare a bag of belongings. But as she later wrote: 'All I wanted was a favourite icon, silver mug and brightly-coloured scarf and Rim.' Unfortunately Rim, a Great Dane, was considered too big to travel. It was 'the first real sorrow of my life... I remember waking early the next morning and racing down with him to the sea and howling in impotent agony at the thought of leaving it all.

'I must have looked very miserable... because they all tried to console me, saying that it would not be for long, that very, very soon we should be back, Rim would still be there and all would be as before. Probably they half believed it, but I knew better...

'Bleakly I spent the morning in errands, carrying envelopes of money to various members of the staff; said my last sobbing goodbye to Rim, then got into the carriage with Granny and Miss King for the drive to Yalta.'

In the course of her short life, little Sofka had spread her social net wide. During her time in the Crimea, she had enjoyed tea with the Dowager, even daring to reprimand her for holding her biscuit in the wrong hand. As a small child at Court, she had played with the young Tsarevich Alexis. At one point the Dolgoroukys had been convinced that little Sofka would make a match for him.

As Sofka's granddaughter wrote: 'Later in life Granny told me that it had been decided that the next Empress had better not be a foreigner and the Child [Sofka herself] was among the suitable candidates and was to be groomed for the post.' But this idea is completely dismissed by the writer Kyril Zinovieff, a relation by marriage of Sofka's: 'Alexis had to marry not only Royalty, but the daughter of a King...'

Sofka also befriended the less suitable grandsons of the

Sofka and Prince Vassily, the 11-year-old playmates

estate's lodgekeeper in the Crimea. Such was her friendship
with these two little revolutionaries that she considered running away and remaining with them. 'I had seen Vanya and
Shura and we had kissed goodbye with the passionate misery of children, but we had no illusions that I would return.
They understood that, while a friend, I still belonged to "the
others".'

The Dolgoroukys' English nanny, Miss King, was a

controversial figure on the *Marlborough* from the start. She argued vociferously with Pridham about where she should sleep and made a fuss about having to sleep close to unfamiliar Russians. Pridham fumed in his diary: 'She did not wish to sleep in any place where Russians might be near her, the only way I could have arranged this would have been by landing fifteen or twenty of them, so she got little sympathy from me.'

An expensive rope of Dolgorouky pearls, worn occasionally by Miss King, failed to offset an otherwise tawdry appearance. As Pridham added with an uncharacteristic lack of gallantry: 'An extremely plain and unpleasant-looking woman, I was tempted to tell her that she was likely to remain unharmed.'

A photograph exists of Miss King with her charge, taken five years before, when Sofka was aged six. The pair are sitting in a sunny garden, Miss King holding a parasol. The confidence and canniness of the child, who leans on Miss King with a broad grin, is in stark contrast to her nanny, who sits upright, her mouth pinched in disapproval.

Miss King's squeamishness towards Russians was fuelled by an equally strong Anglophilia. Sofka, whom she had taught since the age of four, recalled her nanny's eccentricity with some bemusement: 'I had been imbued with the unqualified superiority of all things English – food, manners, clothes, ethics, habits and so on. I had had instilled in me a devout admiration for team games (never having played any), sportsmanship, fair play, "the thing", for a code which was really undiluted Bulldog Drummond.'

As Sofka grew up, she was frequently thrown together with the charges of Miss King's acquaintances: her fellow nannies, Miss New, Miss Young and Miss Blackadder. The nannies all prided themselves on being English; none of them spoke Russian. In fact, the only English nanny who would have spoken any Russian on the *Marlborough* was Miss Coster, an unashamed Russophile, happiest practising her pidgin Russian while enjoying tea from a samovar.

Later in life, Sofka made several attempts to explain her family's employment of Miss King. She pointed out that, at that time, there was a preference at the Russian Court for speaking English. The Tsarina herself preferred to speak English; she found French as much of a struggle as Russian. 'All families had a governess, the difference being that the more up-to-date trend was to have your children speaking English, while the more traditional families clung to French, the universal language of Court.' Nevertheless, why the Dolgoroukys were reduced to Miss King in particular remains a mystery.

Ever since the *Marlborough* had come within sight of the coast, Miss King had been wooing the British officers. Their enthusiastic response can, perhaps, be put down to homesickness. As Sofka wrote: 'Strange delicacies such as Quaker Oats and corned beef appeared on our table. Strange officers always seemed to be coming or going or drinking the tea they brought for Miss King.'

❧

While the ship was anchored at Yalta, 200 tons of baggage was loaded on. The sailors were helped by a detachment of 120 Imperial Army officers. The British officers' accounts dwelt on the hard graft. Pridham wrote in his diary: 'All day embarking more people and tons of luggage! I asked them to obtain as much bedding as they could as I am out to a clinch now.' Commander Fothergill wrote to his sister Punch (Rhoda): 'We were busy the whole day getting gear etc and evacuating to lessen the crowd on various ships.'

It was at this point that Grand Duke Peter's daughter, Princess Nadezhda, embarked, accompanied by her husband Prince Nicholas Orloff. The couple's baby Irina now became the youngest passenger on board. Spotting the new arrivals, Pridham noted in his diary a strong likeness between the Princess and her sister, his helpmate, Marina. Prince Nicholas Orloff, who had served under Nikolasha in the Imperial Guard, spoke fluent English and prided himself on obscure idioms. Pridham was full of admiration: 'Late one evening while he was yarning away in the Wardroom he came out suddenly with the remark: "I must pop off to bye bye". We were greatly amused and offered him our congratulations.'

A curious naval signal was sent at midday from Captain D to the *Marlborough*: 'Request you order *Montrose* to be alongside me by 0700 L.T. tomorrow morning and take the three hundred Poles to Sevastopol their Head Fellow is onshore now.' At ten past twelve a reply was posted: 'Reply. I will do that.'

As it dawned on the passengers that they were going to be at Yalta for a while, several asked the Captain for permission to go ashore. Prince Felix Youssoupov and two other members of the party ended up spending several hours at the port. At one point they were approached by a group of officers who wanted Grand Duke Nicholas, yet again, to take command. They wanted the Grand Duke to accompany them to Novorossisk on a ship with a Russian flag. As members of the Russian Volunteer (White) Army, they would have been wearing distinctive armlets of red, white and blue strips.

Prince Orloff, who prided himself on his knowledge
of obscure English idioms

Unsure what to do, Youssoupov passed the message on
to his mother, Princess Zenaide, upon his return to the ship.
When she in turn spoke to Nikolasha, he swiftly established
that the proposition had no endorsement from the White
Army and dismissed it outright.

The passengers visiting Yalta returned with heartbreaking tales of refugees stranded at the port. Fathers had been
separated from their children, as some ships would take only
men, others only women and children. The crowds jostled
and fought, in fear of their lives. The wounded lay on stretch-
ers amid piles of luggage. In his memoir, Roman recalled
Youssoupov speaking appreciatively of the 'soul strength' of
the British sailors trying desperately to help.

Pridham wrote in anguish that day: 'The people are flock-ing in hundreds to the pier and with only just what they stand up in, the scenes there are indescribable... it is almost impos-sible to control them. In the meantime we have to stand by for a rising of the local Bolsheviks.'

While the *Marlborough* was anchored off Yalta, Xenia received an urgent letter from a family friend pleading the refugees' cause. By now HMS *Grafton*, four British destroyers and one French ship had arrived to help: 'All the refugees are asking for you to intercede... so they will be allowed to remain under English protection and not be left at the mercy of the French. They want to end up on the *Grafton* and in this way to be left in the sphere of your influence on the *Marlborough*. For God's sake help us!'

It was only years later that Xenia was able to reflect more calmly on the proceedings. In her memoirs she includes curi-ous, even humorous, details of the refugees' efforts to gain passage on ships: 'The Russian custom in making long jour-neys is to take lots of cooks along: in exile, especially, chefs took priority over chancellors... so suddenly everybody was claiming to be a chef. Quite a few generals and engineers got aboard that way.'

A sailor from the HMS *Temeraire* kept a diary in which he also noted the extraordinary lengths to which refugees re-sorted in order to get on British ships: 'On deck you meet people of all types, dresses and nations who have decided that they are British at heart, if not by birth, and have come to seek protection. One rather obvious spy had taken the trouble to dress up in bowler hat, gaiters and field glasses.'

Pridham spoke of an endless succession of people coming to the *Marlborough* and begging to be taken away. Though it was clearly a terrible situation, all parties enjoyed the opportunities it offered for lambasting the false-hearted, mutinous French: 'The Empress can do nothing for them [the remaining refugees] it entirely depends on the space we have available in the craft sent here for the evacuation, the French as usual do nothing but hinder, there is general distrust not to say hatred of the French authorities...

'The people trust no-one but the English, it is wonderful to see what faith they have in us, we tell them we will do all that is possible and that, in spite of the fact they have been living in hourly dread of execution or worse for fifteen months, satisfied them, temporarily at any rate.'

Captain Johnson also complained of the French. As the Dowager reported: 'He is indignant with the French for not even having sent ships or done the slightest to help.'

The Dowager herself occasionally wrote critically of the French, but it is still difficult to tell conclusively what her feelings were regarding the French and English. Or indeed which of the two she preferred. When she had first visited England, in 1863, at the time of her sister's marriage to Edward VII, she had been so impressed by the warmth and affection shown the new Queen Alexandra that she had become a frequent visitor.

She had developed a passion for English 'toque' hats which she acquired from the same shop in London as her sister. Her maid of honour reported that when a new hat arrived from London, she would wear it day in day out until it wouldn't hold together any more. She also favoured her sister's London wigmaker. Her eagle-eyed grandson Dmitri was transfixed by her collection of wigs, which, he claimed, accompanied her everywhere in red cardboard boxes. 'Once, as a child, I saw her without her wig and the only hair on her head was a few feathery tufts.'

Those Russians fortunate enough to be already on board the *Marlborough* found themselves in the curious position of being caught up in the panic and yet detached from it. For some, the impulse was to run back into the maelstrom. The Dowager's doughty lady-in-waiting, Countess Mengden, found the impulse irresistible: 'I felt an intense longing coming over me. "Back to my loved ones, if only for a moment!". I succeeded to find a motorboat to take me to Xarax the following morning. There wasn't a jetty there so it was with great effort that the sailors got me ashore by hoisting me up on to the cliff from the boat.

'From there I turned my steps towards Ai-Todor's garden, where I wanted to take a final leave of Shervaschidze's grave and then once more to bid a dear farewell to my brother, his wife and children.

'I drove back to Yalta in a hired car. On the way there we had to go through a wood and here a man suddenly appeared from behind the trees and stopped the car. He jumped up without the slightest hesitation and sat down on the seat opposite me. It was an unpleasant moment. He looked pretty grim so I turned my ring round with a certain caution so that he couldn't see it shine; all the while I jabbered away non-stop so that he didn't have a chance to do anything to me. I thus luckily coped with his company.'

Later in the day, a group of Princes stood on deck, perhaps relishing their blessed position. Prince Roman remembered leaning on the railings with Felix Youssoupov and Xenia's elder sons, Theodor and Nikita. The Princes from Dulber and Ai-Todor had barely known each other in childhood. But, according to Roman, they had forged strong friendships during their incarceration at Dulber.

Youssoupov, he recalled, held a long tube in his hand and

at one point turned to the other Princes saying: 'You'll never guess what this is.' With a theatrical gesture, he informed them that the tube contained two Rembrandt paintings: *Portrait of a Gentleman in a High Hat* and *Portrait of a Lady with an Ostrich Feather.*

In the chaos following the Revolution, he and Irina had returned from the Crimea to spend several weeks at his Moika Palace in St Petersburg. As they were not Romanovs, they had been allowed to travel freely. Before leaving St Petersburg, Youssoupov had taken steps to provide for his family in their uncertain future. First he had hidden gold plate and jewellery: some pieces in secret rooms, others plastered into the walls. He had then cut the Rembrandts from their frames and rolled them in clothes, ready for travel. Upon the couple's return to Koreiz, the paintings were duly hung on a wall, carefully concealed beneath a cousin's altogether less valuable pictures of flowers.

Beside Youssoupov at the rail stood his Abyssinian servant, Tesphe, who held his daughter Irina. Tesphe had been brought back from the young Youssoupovs' honeymoon in Jerusalem. His loyalty to his master was such that for years he had insisted on sleeping outside his room. One of the early excitements of Tesphe's life with the young couple was the discovery of lavatory flushes. He would antagonise would-be bathroom users by spending hours at a time engrossed by the swirling water.

It was suggested – by the Russian courtier Serge Obolensky – that Tesphe prepared the poisoned drinks for Rasputin. But at least one of the conspirators, Vladimir Purishkevich, a member of the Duma, would have opposed the idea of Tesphe's playing such a central role. Purishkevich made it clear that he was horrified by the servant's very presence on the fateful night. It is not known what unnerved Purishkevich about Tesphe, but he was not generally faint-hearted. He had courted controversy by attending the Duma flaunting a derisive red carnation in his fly-button.

In the late afternoon of that first day at Yalta, Roman saw his father, Grand Duke Peter, talking to Nikolasha on deck, when a young *Marlborough* officer approached them, asking to take photographs. Nikolasha agreed, and within the next few minutes 'everyone', as Roman recalled, officers and Russians alike, was reaching for a camera. Pridham himself took pictures; he was a keen photographer, even doing his own developing. While the more retiring Grand Duke Peter opted out of the photo opportunity, Grand Duke Nicholas readily moved to a better light and began striking poses.

That night Nikolasha and his brother Peter discussed their future. It is hard to imagine the tenor of the Grand Dukes' conversation, whether depressed, resigned or even relieved. They had both lived under a sort of sentence of death for two years and now had no idea where they would end up. One thing that they were certain about, however, was that any sort of public life was out of the question. They decided they would live incognito, under the name of Borisowo, the name of a family estate in Minsk.

It had been in May of the previous year that Nicholas and Anastasia had had to sell his estate, Tchair, and move permanently to Dulber. They had sold Tchair to a wealthy industrialist from the Urals. As a result of the Revolution, Nikolasha had lost his income from their estates as well as his regular annual stipend as Grand Duke.

Later that evening, Peter told his son, Roman, that Nikolasha claimed to be wanting nothing more to do with politics. Whether Roman felt that his uncle Nikolasha should

Some of the *Marlborough* passengers, including Grand Duke
Peter, far left, and Vassily, third from the right

withdraw from the public arena is unclear, but he certainly
felt that a quiet life might suit his father, whose most robust
activity was shooting cormorants on the beach.

While the formerly mystical Militsa was present at these
discussions, she seems to have made very little contribution.
For all her much-vaunted gifts of second sight, she was the
only one of the adults insisting that it was far too early to
consider living abroad for ever.

Meanwhile, in the Captain's cabin, the Dowager, evidently
not plagued by thoughts of the future, recorded a satisfactory
timetable: 'We had lunch at 12.30, tea at 4.30 and dinner at
7.30.'

Day 3

The weather changed for the worse. As the Dowager record-ed: 'It is grey, chilly and there is a strong wind, which is a shame... There was a high wind and enormous waves so it was very difficult for the small steamers carrying the luggage etc to moor.' Commander Fothergill also complained to Punch: 'Today there has been rather a bad swell and eventually this afternoon we had to get under weigh to hoist in the boats.'

But the indefatigable Countess Mengden was not to be put off, insisting on braving the waves to get ashore yet again. She described her struggles in her diary: 'The sea became rougher and rougher by the day so that it was quite impossible to use the ship's ladder to get down to the motorboat, which swayed violently up and down. A rope was thrown out from the rail-ing and whoever wanted to go down into the motorboat had to climb down it and try to hit the boat at the very minute the wave lifted it up towards the rope. For me, "landlubber", it seemed to be a hazardous undertaking, but several of the gentlemen and even a couple of the ladies were brave enough to dare try. What can't one get accustomed to?'

The rough sea doubtless exacerbated the passengers' anxiety about the unrest in Yalta. As Commander Fothergill described it to Punch: 'The town is on the verge of rising and the Bolsheviks are only a few miles off.'

'They were arriving at the harbour in crowds,' Pridham wrote, 'some so panic stricken with the news that the Bolsheviks were closing on Yalta that many leaped out of their cars leaving the engines running and stormed down the wharfs in search of a refugee ship.'

And still there were personal pleas to be taken on board from friends of the Imperial Family, for whom passage on a ship would very likely be the difference between life and death. A naval signal arrived that day at 5.00am addressed to the *Marlborough*: 'Princess Bariatinsky and mail with no family has arrived and asked for a boat to go to the *Marlborough*.'

The newly arrived Princess Bariatinsky's son asked the Dowager for permission for his mother and family to come on board. The Dowager agreed without hesitation, clearly forgetting that the days when wishful thinking gave rise to gratification had long gone: 'I agreed as soon as the others Nikolasha and co had left us (I somehow thought that they would go back somewhere).' Unfortunately for the Dowager, Grand Duke Nicholas and his party had no immediate plans to go anywhere.

Over the next few days, she would have found it particularly tantalising as rumours circulated that the Dulbers were about to leave. At least two of these rumours were well founded, originating with the *Marlborough* officers themselves. As it turned out, the Dulbers would indeed disembark well before the Ai-Todors; but not for several days, during which the Dowager's resentment of them would increase.

All in all, as Pridham later noted, the evacuation from Yalta was very arduous indeed, not helped by the chaos prevailing within French ranks. 'We had hastily collected shipping from the Red Sea and Eastern Mediterranean, few of which ships were suitable for carrying passengers, and to the best of our ability met the wishes of the Empress. This was approved by our High Commission in Constantinople because the French Naval vessels in Sebastopol were in a state of complete mutiny, their ships' companies having locked up all their officers and threatened their Admiral if he did not take them all back to France. The French High Commissioner nevertheless accused the British of depriving the French of their rightful responsibility! Typically Gallic.'

A naval signal sent in the morning from D6 to *Marlborough* marks the growing turmoil: 'Should like a Detachment of Marines to assist in keeping crowd off the jetty as there is [sic] about 5000 Greeks trying to get aboard. I have allowed a certain number of the best of them to go onboard our sloops. I am not allowing any more to go.'

The reply from the *Marlborough* is not helpful: 'I cannot land a Detachment of Marines in Boats with the confused sea running in my present Berth.' There was no confusion about a further signal from Sevastopol marked Priority: 'No accommodation for refugees in Sevastopol.'

Amid the upheavals, there lurked a further unspoken threat. Pridham never seems to entertain the idea of the *Marlborough* sailors falling prey to Bolshevik propaganda. But whether this was because he thought such a scenario impossible or simply something he refused to contemplate is hard to know.

The White Russian Chief of Police in Yalta evidently thought it all too possible. He was nicknamed the White Devil because he wore a tall white hat which he said was a protective device: tricking his adversaries into shooting high. The White Devil decreed that any Bolshevik suspected of trying to corrupt foreign sailors would be shot without trial.

He was as good as his word. Pridham reported at least two Bolshevik operatives killed. The first had been trying to recruit a British officer before the White Devil shot him and kicked him into the sea. The second was a woman whom he attempted to shoot while she was dining on a British battleship. 'The Captain, thinking this was all bluff, succeeded in dissuading him from his immediate purpose, insisting that one of HM ships was an unsuitable place for carrying out such a sentence and that in any case he might as well let the lady finish her dinner.'

The lady operative was shot dead as soon as the White Devil could get her off the ship. Pridham acknowledged his unease at the time: 'In those days such summary justice shocked us, but it certainly seemed to have the desired effect since it deterred these agents from approaching the ships embarking refugees.' And such was his loathing of the Reds that he summed up the White Devil, finally, as 'an engaging rogue'.

The Bolsheviks on the streets, meanwhile, naturally ignored the decree; among the choicier incentives they were offering new recruits were, Pridham recorded, aristocrats' wives.

Revolution had been fomenting in Yalta for some time. Immediately after the Revolution in 1917, the Crimean

Regional Social Committee had launched an attack on what was then considered the elitist nature of the citizens of Yalta.

In a sort of call to arms, the Committee had derided Yalta as a monarchist paradise: 'a fabulous place, a healing retreat, surrounded by former Imperial estates and those of his [the Tsar's] kin.' Special efforts were made and stringent measures undertaken to ensure that all those who settled here were 'loyal', not through fear but through their genuine devotion to the Emperor. Only monarchists were allowed to come here to live. For decades a process of 'natural selection' of the population was enforced to guarantee peaceful rest for Nicholas II. No surprise then that he wished to settle at Livadia following his abdication as he was convinced of the loyalty of the inhabitants of Yalta...

It went on: 'This local government has been besieged by complaints of disrespect to the former Imperial Estates: "The common public now stroll in Livadia and Massandra, taking walks and pulling up flowers, often driving through, kicking up dust and disturbing us," these citizens complain. Those who are now arriving in Yalta are the people who formerly could not approach at a stone's throw.'

The Committee was not so much disapproving as bemused by the captive Dowager's new passion for gardening: 'At Ai-Todor Marie Feodorovna has begun occupying herself with horticultural pursuits. She zealously tends to her personal garden where she is cultivating asparagus.'

A Crimean paper, *Krymski Vestnik*, had taken up the baton, complaining about the methods they claimed the Romanovs had used to acquire and keep their properties. The paper accused them of buying up land using the names of people who had died. Further iniquities included prohibiting locals from using the beaches. Finally they had damaged the town's prospects by refusing to allow a railway line to be laid through their estates.

By the spring of 1919, the White Devil's worries about corruption had proven well founded. The Yalta-based Soviet was more hostile than other Soviets towards the Romanovs. More immediately, the streets were littered with hundreds of Bolshevik propaganda leaflets produced by the Moveable Printing Office of the Political Department of the Crimean Red Army.

Addressed to 'English sailors', the leaflets fired questions: 'What base influence forces you to fire at the Revolutionary Russian Army? Don't you see that you fire at your brothers and friends? We are just the same working people as you... you are also working people. All of you have neither castles or factories.'

The leaflets then went on, perhaps unwisely, to allude to the capitulation of the French to the Bolsheviks. The Red Army soldiers could not have known how much the English sailors were enjoying disassociating themselves from the French: 'So it was in Sevastopol where the French sailors, after having visited several times the shore, told Admiral Amette that they wanted to be sent immediately home. More than that they organised a demonstration with red flags and also presented us a red flag.

'They told us that they like us, sympathise with us. Even the French officers and among them the Admiral said that they are against fighting with the Red Army. Now the French sailors are at home.'

The concluding questions on the leaflets were: 'What are you here for? Return home. Have you nothing to do at home? Aren't your wives and children waiting for you?'

White propaganda, carefully conserved alongside the Red

propaganda by Commander Fothergill, was less direct – and rather less literate. Distributed weeks later, it undermined its cause with a litany of infelicities: 'Officers and soldiers of the most powerfull Navy of Great Britain!'... 'During our mutual military labour were difinitly strengthened the fraternal relations between the Russian Army and the Navy of Great Britain. Now we have been persuaded not only by words but by facts, that Great Britain wants to help us quite sincerily and inflexibily and to save the great Russia from the bloody civil war...

'Children of the great country, which is the cradle of political freedom and example of high civism! Take our warmest thanks for your powerfull help, which is coming just at time in our heavy war with the corruptors of our fatherland the bolcheviks – the world's peril! The new Russia will never forget your help.' This was from the Commander of the Voluntary Army of the Crimy and Azoff, General Lieutenant Borovsky.

But in the end, whatever arguments were presented on the streets of Yalta, Pridham's confidence in his men's humanity and sense of fairness was amply borne out. There was widespread sympathy for the White Russian refugees. An officer called Frederick Parker, from HMS *Turquoise*, recalled the situation: 'I was on shore a good deal and got to know and mix with many of the Russians. They were mostly well educated and also nearly penniless (or should I say kopeckless) and a great deal of the sailors' rations went to help the hungry. All the refugees were able to bring with them was jewellery and furs... many sailors reluctantly accepted presents in exchange for such things as soap, sugar etc.'

By the evening, the Yalta police were so alarmed by the prospect of the Bolsheviks' arrival that they asked the *Marlborough* to train its lights on the port. Pridham downplays the emergency but mentions the lights in his diary. 'Things seem to be fairly quiet ashore for the moment, at night we keep a searchlight playing on the town by way of reassuring those who want to leave and subduing those likely to take advantage of the situation.'

Both Pridham and Fothergill mention a visit that evening from Admiral Culme Seymour. His arrival added to the *Marlborough*'s burdens. As Pridham writes: 'The *Lord Nelson* arrived with Admiral Culme Seymour in the evening, this only complicates matters further, as now the Captain must refer everything to him, although the Admiral is not taking charge. A little more luggage came off before the sea got too bad, had to make a good many shifts in the arrangements. News from the Volunteer Army very bad.'

Fothergill mentions that the Admiral brought letters from Queen Alexandra for the Dowager: '...in the evening the weather got better at about 7.20pm the *Lord Nelson* arrived with the Admiral, the Captain went over to see him and brought back a letter from Queen Alexandra to her sister.' The Queen told the Dowager that one of her former ladies-in-waiting, Olga Heyden, had been murdered by the Bolsheviks. 'I cannot say how painful this is', the Dowager confided to her diary.

Roman recorded a poignant conversation during which some of the younger generation of Romanovs discussed going to Poland and Italy. He and Xenia's son, Nikita, seemed to be the only ones present who had no idea what the future held. In August 1918, Nikita's brother Dmitri had written obscurely to Mr Stewart: 'I would like to be in England be with.'

England was one place Prince Roman would assuredly not be going. A gritty correspondence had taken place between Buckingham Palace and the Foreign Office throughout the last few months. Everybody was agreed that, though the Dowager might be welcome, the Grand Dukes would not. One letter from Sandringham read: 'As Lord Curzon is probably aware, the King is strongly averse to any Russian Grand Dukes coming to England under present circumstances.' Another, from the Foreign Office, read: 'there were not the same reasons against the Dowager coming to the country as in the case of the Grand Dukes, whose presence here becomes a source of political embarrassment.'

While discussing the future, no one mentioned one of Xenia's more outlandish ideas: that she and her large family should open a hotel somewhere. Her estranged husband Sandro would be manager, their eldest son Andrei chauffeur, Xenia herself housemaid and all the younger boys lift attendants and porters. Xenia had told her brother, the Tsar, of her plans, in late 1917, and he had written back with enthusiasm: 'I very much enjoyed the plan for setting up a hotel and the allotment of future functions between you, but will it really be in your house?'

Also featured in the plan was Prince Serge Dolgorouky, the Dowager's equerry and Sofka's uncle. Serge, now travelling with the Dowager on the *Marlborough* was, and had been for some time, Xenia's lover. It was his sickly wife's funeral that the Dowager had attended at Koreiz. How he would have regarded his prospective job as doorman at the hotel, particularly with Xenia's husband as manager, cannot be known.

The Dowager favoured her English hats and wigs, and Xenia, too, was well disposed towards England. In 1912 she had taken her children to England for the first time; they had visited Madame Tussauds, spent four weeks at Bognor and, more unusually, enjoyed a visit to Coutts Bank with the ubiquitous Mr Stewart. As Dmitri recalled: 'we were received at the entrance by a lot of sombre gentlemen in frock coats who conducted us to a room, decorated in the Chinese style, which must have been the boardroom.'

Along with Anglophile tendencies, she seems to have nurtured a romantic attachment to an obscure Englishman called Mr Fane. During the First World War, Fane apparently fought with the British Army in France. Xenia had written to the British Royal Family requesting favours on his behalf; she had hoped he'd be sent to Russia on a mission. But after the war, the affair had not been rekindled. During the period of revolution, when friendships and loyalties were pushed to the limit, Xenia had never lost her faith in the British Ambassador, Sir George Buchanan. She had had frequent dealings with him and, shortly after the Revolution, he had defied Provisional Government rules to visit her: 'Grand Duchess Xenia... is quite well though naturally depressed,' he reported peremptorily.

Her sons were very fond of Miss Coster and Mr Stewart, enjoying what they saw as their English eccentricities. While Mr Stewart might initially have seemed less odd than Miss Coster, his eccentricities, when they emerged, were more extreme. On one occasion he wore a kilt. This created so much hilarity, particularly among the servants, that the experiment was never repeated. In St Petersburg he created a further sensation with an electric blanket which he used to offset his 'English custom' of keeping the window open. So enamoured was he of the blankets that he planned to give one to the Tsarina. He abandoned the plan after his own was consumed in a blaze.

The young Princes did meet King Edward VII in Biarritz in 1907 but Dmitri remembered little of him, other than his saying, in a German accent: 'Ach my boys, walk with me.'

As for the servants, they were wary of Europe and Europeans generally. According to Dmitri, they regarded it as a sort of desert: 'Europe was a wild and barren place where few, if any, of the commodities available in Russia could be found. As a result they packed everything they could lay their hands on including coat-hangers and lavatory paper.'

While still at Yalta, Princess Marina received an encouraging naval signal from a mysterious but stalwart Englishman named Jenkins: 'For Grand Duchess Marina Petrovna, HMS *Marlboro*.' Am at Sevastopol en route for Odessa for Constantinople regret extremely to have just missed seeing you and Roman. Good news from our friend in Tiflis. If you have any message for her or if I can assist you in any way write me at our embassy Constantinople. Please send future address. Warmest greetings Jenkins.'

Late that night, the Captain came into the mess and announced that the evacuation was nearly complete; the ship could leave the next day. After the announcement, he added emphatically and doubtless a little stiffly, 'according to the wishes of Her Majesty'.

Roman recalled that it was his parents, Grand Duke Peter and the mystical Militsa, who, with Grand Duke Nicholas, rushed to inform the Dowager of the latest developments. How she would have felt about hearing such important news from the dreaded Dulbers can't be known. She would have suffered the additional blow of dashed hopes as she realised that the Dulbers would not, after all, be disembarking at Yalta.

As the mess emptied, the only figure left was 'Papa

Felix' – Youssoupov's father and the erstwhile Governor of Moscow – who played patience by himself, sitting alone at table. Perhaps, Roman speculated, he wanted to blank out his thoughts.

Day 4

SHIP'S LOG APRIL 10:
AT YALTA
BOATS EMPLOYED TRANSPORTING BAGGAGE
9.30 RA FROM LORD NELSON CAME ON BOARD
13.00 GRAFTON

The last day at Yalta was somehow a triumph of manners. The crew was frantically busy and the passengers distraught, but neither voiced any complaint to the other. Fothergill told Punch: 'This morning it is raining but the wind and swell have gone down. I had to get all the boats out and transport a lot of refugees to the *Grafton*, a lot more have been picked up in sloops and destroyers are evacuating nearly all to Novorossisk, the confounded French having started to evacuate Sevastopol. So tomorrow, or the day after, the Crimea will be Bolshevik. They are only a few miles off this place now I should say we have got off in various crafts around a 1,000 people and their gear!'

Pridham was hampered by the absence, for most of the day, of the Captain. But he made no mention of his travails to the Dowager. She was equally anxious, perhaps out of pride as much as consideration, not to worry Pridham with hers. Pridham writes: 'The Captain was out of the ship nearly all day either with the Admiral or ashore, in his absence I had to do a lot with Her Majesty, however she is very charming. They spend all their time protesting that we do too much for them, which is of course ridiculous. They were greatly impressed with the work of the men in the boats yesterday, who were of course full of beans seeing they had a somewhat distinguished audience.'

Meanwhile, in her diary, the Dowager fretted: 'Great haste and agitation the whole day long since all sorts of alarming news was coming in. The ships no longer dared venture into Sevastopol, so all those unhappy people. who were already there, had to go to Constantinople instead.'

Still more difficult to contain was her increasingly bitter rage with Grand Duke Nicholas and his party's failure to leave the *Marlborough*. Her hopes were repeatedly raised and dashed. Commander Fothergill himself had written in his letter to Punch that the Grand Duke was expected to leave the following day: 'At present we disembark the Grand Duke Nicholas tomorrow to the *Caradoc*, English light cruiser (he's got simply tons of luggage) and that being done probably sail for Constantinople.' But the next day Fothergill informed Punch that the disembarkation had been cancelled later that night.

Fothergill gave no explanation for the change of plan, but it is clear from the Dowager's diary that Nikolasha himself intervened, with his own personal plea to stay on the *Marlborough*. The Dowager vented her disappointment with a sarcastic entry in her diary: 'Nikolasha visited the Admiral on his ship in the afternoon and came back very satisfied and said [that] the Admiral had said he could stay on board here and continue the journey. That was somehow nice!

'I said that it was very awkward as I had invited P[rincess] Bariatinsky with her whole family. He didn't like that at all and only answered that I could tell her that there was no room which was just as impertinent as inconsiderate.'

Although the tenor of such exchanges between the Dowager and Grand Duke was hostile, the pair clearly succeeded in keeping any unpleasantness private, as there is no reference to it in any of the officers' papers, nor in the memoirs of any of the Romanovs.

In her diary, the Dowager bitterly reflected on her impotence: 'My dear gentlemen [Dolgorouky and Viazemski] are of no use or help to me. I have to do everything myself, I, who have previously and all my life been so spoilt.' The Dowager alluded to the 'unpleasant situation' Nikolasha had put her in before concluding furiously: 'Now we are saddled with them [the Dulbers] and can't get rid of them any more.'

In the early afternoon, at 2.14, Captain D sent a stark naval signal to the *Marlborough*: 'Here at last met a capable Russian officer he commands Tartar Regiment. He gives number of troops here as Tartar Regiment 177. Under Commandant of town 100. Independent Volunteers 38. Frontier Company 20. There are as well a party of 40 officers under White Devil who will leave last in small Russian steamer.

'Am taking on board provisions and necessary stores of Tartars and Frontier Company to leave them free to fight. Will embark remainder in destroyers. I think the number of Russian civilians to be evacuated now is exaggerated and besides the Greeks they are not more than 300. The Colonel informs me that their orders are now to go to Novorissisk that Khertch is to be evacuated. Can you verify this for me.'

If the telegrams were confusing, the fact remained that, in the end, the Dowager had succeeded in her plea to be the last to leave. As one of her ladies-in-waiting, Countess Yekaterina Kleinmichel, put it: 'Instead of the rest of the squadron allowing HMS *Marlborough* with the Empress on board to sail first, it was She who, like a mother, covered the retreat of Her children.'

Elizabeth Zinovieff, who escaped on a British ship, also paid tribute to the Dowager's efforts: 'In this way the Empress Marie undoubtedly saved a substantial part of the nobility of Russia and we must be grateful to her for the rest of our lives for without her we should undoubtedly have been killed.'

Though almost all the refugees were rescued by the English, there were some rescued by French stragglers. Elizabeth Zinovieff's brother, Alexander, found himself on a French ship with sailors, presumably Bolshevik sympathisers, who refused to start the engine. Eventually Alexander and his officer friends were obliged to stoke up the ship themselves.

But those lucky enough to escape from Yalta avoided further misery. The town swiftly deteriorated into a battleground, with first the Reds, then the Whites taking charge. Marc Wolf, then a young lawyer in Yalta, remembered listening in amazement as Bolshevik officials argued about whether theft was a crime. He remembered a Red-affiliated band dressed in women's fur coats, wearing ammunition as decoration.

The atrocities committed by the Whites more than matched those of the Reds. Wolf resolved to leave after witnessing the Whites' hanging of a 17-year-old boy simply because he shared Trotsky's surname, Bronstein. Serge Obolensky remembered corpses of Reds hanging on the wire supporting rose bushes in the gardens of one of the estates.

That evening on the *Marlborough* an event took place which moved all those who witnessed it, sailors and aristocrats and servants alike. Most of the Romanovs were on deck and the Dowager and Nikolasha were engaged in conversation, perhaps discussing the unfortunate Bariatinskys and their failed attempt to get on board. Just then a ship passed, carrying members of the Dowager's guards; at the sight of the Dowager and the Grand Duke, the soldiers began to sing the Russian National Anthem.

Fothergill, moved in spite of himself, described the moment in a letter to Punch that evening: 'The Empress's bodyguard left just now in a sloop for Sevastapol. They are composed of about 170 officers who have been guarding her, all volunteers left from the old army – the sloop steamed round us and they all stood to attention and saluted and cheered her as they passed, rather a touching sight.'

Roman spoke of the deep impression left on all those who had witnessed the moment, adding that Nikolasha saluted the officers and the Dowager made the sign of the cross. Prince Dmitri, who was not given to exaggeration, later wrote: 'Everyone, including the British crew, were in tears.' His younger brother Vassily was no less moved as, years later, he conjured up the scene: 'My grandmother standing alone, smiling sadly; the Grand Duke standing also alone, very tall and magnificent and then hearing the sound of the beautiful Russian National Anthem.

'I was standing on the deck with my cousin. He was a man and I was a boy of 11, but we both had the same feelings. Tears came to our eyes and he turned to me and said with a smile: "What fools we are". I'll never forget that.'

At the close of his first memoir, *Lost Splendour*, Prince Felix Youssoupov made the most of the poetry of the occasion; he alone mentioned the Dowager's tears. 'The *Marlborough* had not yet weighed anchor; standing in the bow, the Empress watched the ship pass by. Tears streamed down her cheeks as these young men, going to certain death, saluted her.'

The Dowager also described the scene. Tellingly, she wrote about it the following day, the previous day's entries being full of rage against Nikolasha: 'I forgot to say yesterday that all our poor officers from the Okhrana were put onboard an English ship at my request and were sailing in great silence round our ship when they suddenly starting cheering and did so for as long as we could see them. It was frightfully moving, just as lovely as it was touching but for us indescribably sad.' Curiously, in common with Youssoupov, she doesn't mention the anthem; perhaps the officers only

The Empress on the deck of the *Marlborough*, receiving the salute from members of the Imperial Guard as they left Yalta

managed a few bars, amid the cheering.

Her mood was not missed by Pridham. He wrote: 'Until long after the sloop had passed there was silence. No one approached the Empress, while she remained standing, gazing sadly after those who, leaving her to pass into exile, were bound for what seemed likely to be a forlorn mission. Few are known to have survived the next period of fighting Bolsheviks outside Sevastopol.'

At the time he noted in his diary: 'A pathetic scene on board here and not too pleasant to witness; nearly all of those in the sloop are either closely related to someone on board here or have lived alongside them all their lives, the entire detachment being officers. In one ship they were going to exile, in the other to what will probably prove to be certain death.'

The Dowager concluded her diary entry for the day peremptorily: 'The Captain dined with us.'

Day 5

SHIP'S LOG APRIL 11:
FROM YALTA TO PRINKIPO
08.00 PREPARING FOR SEA
HOISTED BOATS.

On April 11th at 8.30am, the ship was finally under way for Constantinople: 'rather a cold and dull day,' Fothergill reported starkly. The morning began, as usual, with the two national anthems – English and Russian – being played on deck. The Romanovs had all been struck by this particular gesture. Youssoupov mentioned the anthems in his memoir: 'in the morning we were up early to attend the colours at which English and Russian hymns were played.' The Dowager described how the anthems were played as the flag was hoisted: 'the first time I was so emotional that I could not restrain my tears.'

The Dowager's faithful Cossack guard Timofei Yachik later wrote that, on the morning of their departure, the Dowager was full of hopes for the future: 'on that day Empress Dagmar was absolutely convinced that soon she would see the Tsar.'

She was in fact accompanied on the *Marlborough* by two Cossacks, both heavily bearded and well over six feet. They kept 12-hour watches and would lie across the threshold of her bedroom door. An English ADC who looked after the Dowager later on in her journey said he always knew where she was, because there would be a conscientious Cossack close by.

Timofei Yachik, who celebrated his 41st birthday on the *Marlborough*, had been with the Dowager for four years. A lifelong monarchist, he had left the Kuban region, aged 22, to put his considerable weight behind the Tsar at the Caucasus front. He had then apparently been happy to seal himself off with the Dowager at the Russian Court, barely seeing a wife and two daughters. One of his peculiarities was that he insisted on having a giant knife, fork and spoon specially made for him: he found regular cutlery too fiddly.

But however well Timofei felt he knew the Dowager, his reading of her mood as she caught her last glimpse of the Crimean coast was overly optimistic. In fact, judging by her diary, the strength of her emotions would have allowed little space for thoughts of the future: 'I got up early, before we weighed anchor. I had just come up when we sailed past the flagship where music was playing. It was heartbreaking to see that lovely coastline slowly disappear behind a thick fog, which hid it from our eyes for the last time.'

Little Princess Sofka always remembered her last view of the turrets of Ai-Todor. She later wrote that she saw her departure from the Crimea as marking the end of her childhood.

Prince Roman, confusingly, gives a moving description of leaving at night. He wrote that he heard the anchor being lifted, then watched from the deck, just discerning the light-

The Dowager's trusty Cossacks, who kept 12-hour watches
lying across the threshold of her bedroom

house at Ai-Todor and the walls of Dulber in the last rays
of the sun. He wrote in his memoir that he kept a diary, so
possibly the entry was wrong. He may have retained a strong
impression of the preceding night and then not been up in
time to see the morning departure. 'The HMS *Marlborough*
took us away from the Russian coast towards the Bosphorus.
It became night.'

As the ship pulled away, a poignant exchange took place

between Captain Johnson and Xenia. He had lent Xenia his binoculars. She said, 'What are all those little black things glittering along the shore?' His reply was stark: 'Madame, that is your silver.'

The servants had been so worried they would be abandoned, that they had kept several cases back, refusing to load them onto the boats. About 54 cases were left on the quay. Xenia told the Captain that the cases did not matter, but, over the coming years, she would regret their loss. Vassily later said that the servants only realised at the last moment that they would not be left behind. At that point they felt the best thing they could do was leave the cases open, so other refugees could help themselves.

By the time the *Marlborough* left Yalta, it was carrying treasures worth an estimated £20 million. Along with the Rembrandts, the Youssoupovs had a stash of jewellery carefully concealed within Zenaide's luggage. Grand Duke Peter and Militsa had left the family's silver in St Petersburg but managed to bring the 'secondary silver' used by the butler below stairs. Along with his family plate, Nikolasha had brought his Sword of Honour with a gold hilt studded with diamonds. The *Marlborough*'s 'manifest', which would have given details, is not available at the Public Records Office. But an approximate valuation can be gleaned from subsequent reports of sales, thefts and 'con' tricks.

In fact, the treasure left on the Yalta quay would have made poor currency for its finders; it emerged subsequently that British sailors were being offered diamond rings for just half a crown. On sixpence pay a day, providing they forewent extra eggs, bread and porter, the sailors could have raised cash for such a ring in five days.

Pridham retired to his cabin to write again. The Empress

had confided her worries about the refugees unable to accompany her on the *Marlborough*: 'The departure from Yalta was another of those pathetic scenes of which we have seen too many recently. In spite of her own feelings, the Empress was up to the last moment only concerned with the safety of the people who were not fortunate enough to be in this ship.

'The question of accommodating the refugees is a very difficult problem, no country wishes to be saddled with them, they have nothing with which to support themselves and in many cases are too old to work. Hence the accusation of criminal folly against France for not holding the Crimea.'

He consoled himself with one optimistic reflection about Communism. 'There is only one bright spot on the horizon and that is the fact that Bolshevism, consisting as it does of Evil only, cannot triumph in the end.' His prediction would, of course, prove right; but not for some 70 years.

Returning to the concerns of the day, he worried about the effect of the weather on his passengers. On that first day of their journey, the passengers found themselves forced to retreat to their cabins as they were engulfed, perhaps appropriately, in a sort of London pea-soup fog: 'Fog did not add much to the comfort of the passengers this afternoon, they can only be in very stuffy cabins down below or on deck.'

In his memoir, he recorded the first moments at sea and the crew's not very successful efforts to make the passengers comfortable: 'We tried to screen part of the quarter-deck from the wind, but this provided little shelter and the constant shower of "stokers" (smuts) from the funnels of our coal burning boilers, which eddied about the deck with that aggravating and at times painful propensity for lodging in the eye, drove them below.'

The Black Peril, who chose to spend much of their five-day journey in their cabins, would have felt additionally restricted by the fog. They may have spared a thought for their French psychic, Philippe Vachot. Monsieur Philippe, whom they had brazenly introduced to the Russian Court, had distinguished himself as a master of the weather. He had quelled breezes on dusty parade grounds and once even tempered storms impeding the progress of the Tsar's Royal Yacht *Standart*.

As the fog and wind showed no sign of letting up, Pridham was impressed by the passengers' cheerful stoicism. But it only served to highlight the shortcomings of the one grumbler on board: Sofka's irrepressible English nanny, Miss King. Her nationality, of which she was so proud, would have been an additional blow for Pridham. Miss King, as it turned out, was not particularly worried about the elements, but she was nursing a host of other grievances. 'Miss King arrived almost at the last moment and has made herself extremely objectionable ever since...

'Miss Coster, the other English governess, has always been ready to do everything possible to help things along. This other creature... is a badly bred, unhealthy looking person with a distinctly alcoholic nose.

'One of the first things she did was to make unpleasant remarks about some of the people on board.' (Pridham later specified that she was rude about the Imperial Family and Russia in general). 'I am rather glad she did, as I knew how to deal with the matter when I saw her holding forth to some sailors; she is no longer permitted such opportunity.'

In his memoir, he implies that there was continuing bad feeling between him and Miss King or, as he discreetly calls her, 'an objectionable Englishwoman'. This was doubtless owing to the measures he took to silence her: 'Needless to say steps were taken to prevent a repetition of this incident and I am glad to say these angered hei greatly.' He mused in his diary. 'I fail to understand how this type of person gets taken into a situation like hers.'

Meanwhile, the Dowager, having dealt with the agonies of the departure, seemed to set her mind to counting her blessings. She was rhapsodic about her present circumstances, making no comment about having, for the moment, to eat with and talk to the Dulbers: 'I live in Capt Johnson's cabin, sleep in his lovely bed and enjoy a lovely drawing room where we sit after meals and where some of the boys and Pavlik Fersen sleep at night.

'At meal times my neighbours are mainly Nikolasha and Petiusha – Grand Duke Peter – alternating with Papa Felix. The Black Sisters remain seated after dinner and converse with me till about 11 or, if they leave earlier, we play patience with the Youssoupovs.' After years at Court, the black sisters were clearly as practised as the Dowager at maintaining a show of good relations.

During the day, the Dowager was comfortably set up by the crew in a corner next to the gun towers. Here she spent long periods reclining on deckchairs with the companions of her choice: Youssoupov's mother, Princess Zenaide, and Sofka's grandmother, Baroness Dolgorouky. They were occasionally visited by little Prince Vassily, who, according to Roman, amused them with his tricks. Vassily was always reputed to be his 'Amamma's' best-loved grandchild.

He had been a favourite at Court, selected as icon boy for the wedding of his sister Irina to Felix Youssoupov. Because of hostilities between the Youssoupovs and the Tsarina over Rasputin, the wedding had taken place at the Dowager's palace. Dmitri had been somewhat put out by his younger brother's venture into the limelight. He had found Vassily's glamorous ride on a golden coach drawn by four white horses particularly galling, and gave him a damning report: 'He walked very badly and would stop and look around at the guests who were lining the rooms so the Emperor was obliged to flick him with his fingers on his ear to make him keep pace with the procession.'

In the course of the ceremony, Vassily had further disgraced himself by finishing the remains of the champagne in the guests' glasses, then stumbling and falling while getting into the car. According to Dmitri, the Tsar set the ball rolling by giving Vassily his half-filled glass. 'Later I saw him finishing other glasses around the room and he eventually had to be removed from the party by Nana Coster.' In an interview in 1984 Vassily summed up the occasion with brio: 'That was my first salute to Bacchus.'

Nevertheless, the ceremony had gone well, by and large, with bride and groom triumphing over several bad auguries, not least Youssoupov getting trapped in a lift and Irina selecting a tiara once worn by Marie Antoinette.

Adversity had brought the Dowager and her two elderly companions particularly close. Princess Zenaide's sorrows had begun years earlier with the death of her elder son, Nikolai, in a duel. Since the death, she had been beset with bouts of depression. Following the Revolution, all three women underwent further travails.

The Dowager, in particular, now had to face the possibility that she had lost her two surviving sons and five of her grandchildren. Her sorrow regarding the past was matched by apprehension about the future. While she was bound initially for England, where would she eventually end up? If she really believed the Tsar and his family had survived, she must have been deeply worried about what would become of them.

As the three sat commiserating with each other, they may have derived comfort from apportioning blame for their troubles. The Black Sisters and the Tsarina would obviously have been called to account, but their prime culprit would undoubtedly have been Rasputin or, as the Dowager called him, 'the dubious individual'. By the time the Dowager had moved to Kiev, Rasputin's charisma was so strong that ladies collected his nail clippings and sewed them into their underwear.

Down in the Crimea, Princess Zenaide had been given short shrift by the Tsarina when she continued to voice her disapproval of Rasputin. The Tsarina had retorted: 'It is a plot against a dear friend and nobody has the right to interfere. You can leave.' That evening Zenaide had been persuaded to meet the Tsarina at dinner. One of her fellow guests, a baroness, recalled Zenaide as 'pale and trembling'. The well-meaning baroness hoped to smooth things over when she saw that one of the Tsarina's cushions had slipped down: *"Allez ma chère, remasser ce coussin; offrez-le à l'Imperatrice; cela peut être rompera la glace"*. But the Princess with a terrified look answered, *"Ma bonne amie, jamais je n'oserais"*.'

However, Zenaide eventually recovered her mettle, merrily criticising Rasputin in letters to her son. Because of the censorship, she would refer to Rasputin facetiously as the 'Book', short for the Bible.

Zenaide would have been aware that, in the end, the Tsarina had a flawed armoury. No amount of steel could compensate for her unpopularity. Years later, her nephew Prince Dmitri said of his aunt laconically: 'looking back I would say she had bad fluids.'

Just before Rasputin's murder, Youssoupov had told his wife Irina of his plan in a barely intelligible letter; she had replied by return of post: 'Dear Felix, Thank you for your insane letter. I could not understand the half of it. I realise that you are about to do something wild. Please take care and do not get mixed up in any shady business.'

But, for all Irina's protestations, Prince Dmitri later wrote that his sister had understood exactly what was going on, and approved of it. He had been with her in the Crimea on that fateful night and reported that she had received a telegram at 4.00am: 'It's all over.'

Shortly after the murder, Zenaide had publicly voiced support for her son, sending an uncompromising message to Xenia. She began by offering thanks to Xenia's husband, Sandro, for defending Felix and begging immunity for him.

Within days of the party's embarkation on the *Marlborough*, Pridham had been brought round to the ladies' point of view. 'That the Emperor had appointed and followed the advice of unprincipled Ministers had become evident to all, even perhaps to the Emperor himself. It was here that the evil and insistent influence of Rasputin, fanatically urged upon him by his Empress as heaven-sent counsel, proved to be the main factor in the downfall of the dynasty.'

For the ladies on deck, the Black Peril would, of course, have provided rich pickings. How could they forgive them for remaining, cuckoo-like, on the *Marlborough*? How could they ever have been expected to deal with their more extreme eccentricities? It was, after all, Zenaide's husband, the elder Prince Felix, who had once spotted Militsa riding in a carriage and been bemused when she had failed to respond to his wave. When the Prince challenged her, a few days later, she said he could not possibly have seen her since she was with the psychic Monsieur Philippe, 'and when he wears a hat he is invisible and so are those with him'.

Below deck, the 'crows' as they were also known, would have been tending to their own regrets. The once formidable sisters had lost every aspect of their power and were now expected, along with the other refugees, to be grateful for their very lives. It is not known how they felt about their prospects and whether they knew that they were not welcome even in England.

In their glory days, in the early 1900s, they had taken pleasure in pulling rank, insisting on their right to follow immediately behind the Tsar, Tsarina and Dowager. As Grand Duchess Xenia's sister Olga put it: 'The sisters were nicknamed Scylla and Charybdis and nobody dared to make a move until the Montenegrin ladies were where they considered they should be.' Their influence at Court had been such that, once, when the Tsarina had a stomach disorder, the sisters were permitted to dispatch all the doctors and tend to her themselves.

Among their first projects had been the introduction of the self-vanishing Monsieur Philippe to the Tsar and Tsarina during the Imperial couple's visit to France. At first he had been a great success, encouraging the Tsar to practice spiritualism and table-turning. The Tsar had made the most of these sessions, gleaning advice from his late father, the fork-bending Alexander III. It was only when Monsieur Philippe's promise to produce an heir failed and the Tsarina was exposed as having no more than a phantom pregnancy, that he was unceremoniously dismissed.

Relations between the sisters and their most successful protégé, Rasputin, once soured, never recovered. This despite Rasputin's having, at one point, been obliged to take refuge at

Militsa's palace while on the run from the police, who were trying to serve up a decree banishing him from St Petersburg for five years. They found Rasputin on the station platform, then chased him to the palace, where he remained for a full three weeks.

Militsa may have been prepared to help her former protégé in extremis but she had not forgiven him. Indeed, she felt extremely ill-served by him and had no compunction about contributing to the damning report wordily entitled 'File of the Tobolsk Consistory in the Charge against Grigory Efimovich "Rasputin-Novy" a Peasant of the village of Pokrovskoe in the Tyumen District of Spreading of False Khlyst-like Doctrine and of Forming a Society of Followers of His False Doctrine. Opened 6 September 1907'. The concluding accusation of the file denounces him as full of 'self-importance and Satanic pride'.

By 1913, the sisters had entirely lost favour at Court. Their initial championing of Rasputin had damaged them for ever in the eyes of the Dowager; their subsequent accusations against him had outraged the Tsarina. Princess Zenaide wrote to her son Felix, describing a dinner party at the Tsar's Crimean estate, Livadia: 'The black sisters walk about like people stricken with the plague. None of the courtiers will even go up to them, seeing that the hosts ignore them completely.'

The sisters' isolation on the *Marlborough*, as they remained below deck, emerging only for meals, was almost as severe. Prince Roman, noting his mother's and aunt's absence, preferred to accept at face value their continuing plea of ill health.

In the evening, Pridham asked Commander Fothergill to invite Grand Duke Nicholas to dine with them 'unofficially', as he put it. Both officers were under the impression, wrongly as it turned out, that the Grand Duke was leaving the ship the following day at Constantinople and that this would therefore be his last night on board. They agreed that it would be sad to miss this final opportunity to enjoy his company. To Fothergill fell the privilege of raising the toast: 'I asked him... if he would honour us by dining in the Ward Room, he seemed very pleased and the dinner was a great success... he [Nikolasha] sat on my right, rather a trial as he can only talk French.

'However he was very interesting and after I had proposed the health of the Empress and all the Russian Royal Family he got up and made a simply ripping speech. After dinner he gave us a long account of his campaigns and presented a very fine signed photograph to the mess.'

At the end of his speech, Grand Duke Nicholas in turn raised a toast to absent comrades of the *Marlborough* officers. Fothergill kept a typed copy of the Grand Duke's words. In neat handwriting at the top he has written 'Copy of Speech made by the Grand Duke Nicholas of Russia at dinner given in Ward Room office HMS *Marlborough* at sea Yalta to Constantinople April 11th 1919'.

Messieurs, Je vous remercie au nom de ma famille pour l'hospitalité que vous nous avez offerte à votre bord. Cette hospitalité est allée droit a nos coeurs – veuillez me croire que notre reconnaissance vient aussi du plus profond de nous-meme. Messieurs! Souvenez-vous que ce ne sont pas de vaines paroles, mais celles d'un vieux soldat. Je vous donne ma parole que ni ma famille ni moi n'oublierons jamais la

manière dont nous avons été recus tant que nous serons en
vie. Nous sentons bien la sincerité de vos bons sentiments
pour nous, et c'est ce que nous touche le plus. Permettez-moi
de lever mon verre à la sante du Commandant de Marl-
borough et de tous ses officiers – dites a vos camarades que
sont absents au service que je bois à leur santé et combien je
regrette de na pas les avoir rencontrés à cette table.

Pridham was equally enraptured. How he handled his twin
passions for the feuding Dowager and Grand Duke is unclear.
He must have passed on to the Dowager his increasing admiration for the Grand Duke. She presumably managed a sufficiently gracious reponse and kept her views on the limits of
Grand Duke Nicholas's intellect to herself.

Pridham's diary entry was unequivocal: 'It was a great
success. He made a most wonderful speech in French. It is no
wonder he can lead men when he gets an opportunity to talk
to them. They say that had he acted at once at the beginning
of the Revolution he could have stopped it; being approached
on the subject, he eventually decided that he could only do it
at the cost of very great bloodshed; little knowing that this
was to happen ten-fold if he did not act.'

The animosity of both sailors and refugees towards the
French was second only, it now emerged, to their loathing
of the Germans. Pridham refers in his diary to 'the hand of
Germany' as the 'tool of Satan', adding, with approv-
al 'Grand Duke Nicholas will hardly mention the word
'German' and, upon being shown a Hun bayonet, a present
to the Mess from one of the soldiers who visited us when we
were in the Grand Fleet, refused to touch it.'

Given the moral battering Nikolasha had suffered in the
years since the Revolution, there is something poignant about

his choice of gift to the *Marlborough* officers; and something equally touching about the simple manner in which it was received. 'Before he left the Mess he presented us with, as he called it, "his card", a very fine photograph of himself in Cossack uniform.' It is clear from his posture as well as his facial expression that the Grand Duke, previously so ready to pose on deck, knew he was photogenic.

Pridham was as satisfied with the Grand Duke's photograph as with some of his more obviously appealing gifts: 'We have had two presents in the shape of cases of Crimean wine from the Royal Estates. The Grand Duchess Xenia and Prince Youssoupov (sen) gave these, we propose to reserve them for special occasions.'

That first night at sea, Youssoupov gave an impromptu guitar concert in the hold. He set great store by his musicianship. By all accounts he was indeed quite accomplished – able to disseminate sorrow, high spirits or even calm with his Russian gypsy songs. He had played to Rasputin on the night of his murder. Rasputin, for all his psychic powers, had clearly not picked up on any of the tension in the atmosphere. He had made a simple request: 'Play something cheerful; I like listening to your singing.'

When an unruly band of Bolsheviks had stormed Koreiz, attempting to arrest his father, Youssoupov had stepped into the breach. Later he described two of his adversaries with relish: 'one wore a diamond bracelet, the other a brooch. Their uniforms were stained with blood.' Though the marauders were slightly mollified by the news that Youssoupov had murdered Rasputin, the real spirit of accord began after they spotted his guitar. 'I sang several songs and they joined in the choruses. One bottle after another was emptied and our guests got more and more boisterous... the sailors finally went off after shaking hands with us again and again... the whole band jumped into their saddles, waved farewell in the most friendly fashion and brandishing their flags (marked: "Death to the bourgeois", "Death to the landlords") disappeared into the hills.'

This first concert on board was marked by the unexpected appearance of the Dowager. Youssoupov had, for some time, been struck by her changes of mood which were, he noted, 'childishly mercurial': one minute laughing to herself at some private joke, the next minute engulfed in a stream of uncontrollable tears. It was, of course, Youssoupov who had particularly noted her tears the previous evening as she listened to the doomed White officers singing the national anthem.

Now he recalled how gratifyingly moved she was by his singing: 'Our group of young gathered amongst the trunks and cases which served as seats. At the behest of our friends, I brought out my guitar and sang gypsy songs. Suddenly a door opened and we saw the Empress. She made a sign to me not to stop and sat down on a trunk, listening in silence till the end of my song. Lifting my eyes toward hers, I saw hers filled with tears.'

The Dowager had always been particularly susceptible to music. Prince Dmitri recalled: 'My grandmother had a device installed at the Anitchkov Palace, her St Petersburg residence, through which one could listen to performances at the Maryinsky, a distance of some mile or so away. A tube with several extensions was installed in one of the drawing rooms and this ran underground to the theatre where it came out alongside the stage. The device was quite effective – one simply removed the cord and put the receiver to one's ear.'

By the end of the *Marlborough* voyage, Youssoupov had

succeeded in the more challenging task of beguiling the British officers. Pridham was impressed: 'One evening he entertained a few of the officers with some Russian folk songs, to the accompaniment of his guitar, which he sang and played delightfully.'

In the course of that first day of their journey into exile, all the refugees were issued with certificates. Xenia's read: 'I certify that HIH Grand Duchess Xenia Alexandrovna left Russia in HMS *Marlborough* on the 11th April 1919. (signed) Capt. Johnson.'

The author Kyril Zinovieff, who knew many of the *Marlborough* passengers later in their lives, now says that, from the moment of their departure from their native land, refugees inhabit a sort of abstract state of their own: 'Being a refugee is a nationality: Refugeeland. Refugeestan. There's no need to start explaining to other refugees how you feel about being a refugee. What refugees discuss permanently is their memories.'

Day 6

Waking up at sea, out of sight of their homeland, represented a further wrench for the refugees. The sanguine saw it as the beginning of a new life, the melancholy saw the end of everything they held dear. Their opposing moods informed their accounts, resulting in discrepancies even on basic descriptions of weather and landscape.

They would all have been in superficial agreement, however, on the fog which once more engulfed the ship through the night and early morning. Fothergill mentioned its preventing the ship getting to the Bosphorus till about 10.00am. In his bald account he described the *Marlborough* as going past Constantinople and finally anchoring at Prinkipo (one of the Prince's Islands). The Dowager noted that 'Unfortunately we had a bad fog in the evening so that we had to move very slowly and the siren hooted every minute the whole night long.'

She was disappointed by the Dardanelles: 'It was unfortunately grey and overcast, very damp so that the pretty approach through the Dardanelles did not make the lovely impression it should have done, which was a great pity. We just sailed through and dropped anchor at the Prince's Islands, which are not especially lovely. We were all up to admire the coast and arrived at 11.00 o'clock. Here we saw several ships packed full with all our poor refugees, who had arrived yesterday... It was windy and not at all warm.'

Youssoupov, in *En Exil*, described their journey entirely differently. 'The Bolphorus appeared to us under a sky like a grand finale, lit up with shining rays, while behind us, like a sombre curtain drawn over our past, heavy clouds of storm barred the horizon.'

Pridham also took a buoyant view: 'Very great interest was shown by the passengers, few of whom had been through before. Had a very busy day, what with paravanes to be got out and in, escorting various parties to places in the ship from which they could get a good view of the scenery, anchoring and then a stream of visitors.'

Prinkipo was the largest of the nine Prince's Islands in the Sea of Marmara and lay 12 miles from Constantinople. Though the Dowager failed to see its attraction, Prinkipo was generally regarded as a picturesque holiday destination. Ten years later, in 1929, an unlikely fellow Russian exile, Trotsky, settled on the island after being banished from the Soviet Union. He lived there for four years.

Perhaps the Dowager's view was tainted by the thought of Prinkipo's beleaguered refugees. Hundreds of Russians were now marooned on the island, suffering from a lack of food, water and proper sanitary arrangements. They had undergone a particular humiliation when Turkish officials insisted that all clothes be fumigated. Xenia's sister, Grand Duchess Olga, who was subject to the same strictures, reported: 'They [the clothes] needed it, but that rough and ready process did not improve their appearance and our footwear shrank most horribly.'

As the ship anchored at Prinkipo, there was still some confusion as to where many of the *Marlborough* refugees were to be taken. The Dowager remained convinced that this was a likely disembarkation juncture for the Dulbers, and would have been horrified to know that, at this stage, some British authorities were as yet under the impression that the two prickly parties were expected to continue their journey into exile together.

It was as well she was not privy to telegrams which failed to mention the Dulbers' long-promised departure. The *Marlborough* officers who had been expecting the Dulbers to disembark had, it appeared, been misinformed.

Malta now began to be mentioned as a destination. In the early evening, a secret telegram was sent to the Governor of Malta from the British diplomat Lord Milner, Colonial Secretary, 'S. of S., Colonies', saying that all the passengers were to be disembarked at Malta. The Governor was informed that the party was impoverished and was to be received without ceremony: 'HMS *Marlborough* due at Constantinople today is proceeding to Malta arriving probably on Tuesday to land the following persons who are on board: Empress Marie, the Dukes Nicholas and Peter, their wives, families and suite making altogether 25 to 30 people.

'Please receive them with as little ceremony as possible and unofficially, and you had better not meet them yourself. They will arrive practically destitute without clothes or money. Pending decision as to where they are to go, temporary accommodation will be required, but it is not considered desirable to house them where the Governor is in residence. His Majesty suggests San Antonio may be available. Do not allow arrival or any references to it to appear in the local papers. All proper expenses of maintenance and clothing will be refunded to you... Milner.' Secrecy was essential because the Romanovs were still regarded as politically incendiary.

That night the Governer of Malta decided it would be politic to go ahead with a planned trip to the opera. But preparations were begun immediately to clear his residence, the San Antonio Palace, for the Dowager. The Governor's ADC, Captain Robert Ingham, later reported that he received an urgent instruction from the Governor: 'I wish you to have the Palace cleared of all our things. Get new crockery, linen, blankets and everything necessary and I will leave all the best silver and glass for you.'

The Governor of Malta's reply to the Colonial Secretary, Milner, was terse. He complained about the ever changing arrangements: originally the party was to arrive on the 14th, then the 15th and comprise 30 people in total. 'Imagine my feelings on finding, on my return to Valletta, the *Marlborough* would not arrive until 20th or 22nd with a cargo of 30 Royalties and 31 retainers.' On a semi-jocular note, he added: 'I have placed 40 dozen 1906 Champagne (bought for the succeeding Governor) under lock and key for I have no confidence in the statement that Russians have taken the pledge!'

One of the problems facing the ADC in Malta was that everybody wanted to know why the Governor's family was vacating the San Antonio Palace; they had just arrived from another palace and had unpacked for a three-month stay.

Ingham explained his difficulty to the Governor: 'Lord Methuen replied that I need not actually tell a lie but if anybody asked me for an explanation I could murmur the word "DRAINS". We had no trouble after that.'

A further telegram to Admiralty from the Commander in Chief Mediterranean later in the evening gave what would turn out to be a more accurate picture of the party's fate. It is evident from this telegram that the Grand Dukes were now not expected to go to Malta. The telegram spoke of 'the Grand Duchess Xenia and her family who will accompany Empress to England also Grand Dukes Nicholas and Peter with their wives and families and entourage who propose to disembark Constantinople and whose future movements have not yet been decided'.

The *Marlborough* officers accepted that, for now, there would be a sort of stalemate. As Fothergill told Punch: 'We shall probably stay here [Prinkipo] till tomorrow night or until the Government decide where we are to land these people.'

But for the moment, three days after embarking the party, Pridham had more immediate concerns: the ship's food supply was dwindling. The combination of stress, boredom and months of deprivation had increased the appetites of the passengers. For two years they had all lived in fear of their lives; even after their rescue from the Crimea, most of them still had no idea where they were going. Kyril Zinovieff years later recalled the preoccupation the refugees had with food: 'For my parents' generation the memories were about food... they would remember how it trickled down.'

Youssoupov made a wry allusion to the passengers' preoccupation in his memoir: 'The appetite of his passengers was a source of worry to the Captain. He feared he was going to have to watch provisions meant to last several weeks disappear in a few days.'

Pridham had certainly been taken by surprise: 'The Commander-in-Chief came off with some of his staff. Had to give the Flag Commander all the details of the party and arranged that he should obtain a supply of food for us, the last few days have rather taxed our resources, fortunately the Captain had laid in a wonderfully good store and an excellent "cellar".' Or, as he put it more decorously in his memoir: 'The C-in-C had anticipated our need and soon after anchoring supplies arrived and an anxious Captain's steward breathed again.'

The following day Fothergill complained to Punch of the expense: 'just imagine what things are like here, sent ashore for food last night and the bill came this morning. 24 cauliflowers for £6!' Pridham complained further of the confusion surrounding the currency. One pound, usually ten roubles, was now 60 to 100 roubles. Rouble notes varied in value: those issued before 1909 were the most valuable, and the current denomination, called 'domskies', worth least. He added later that by the following year one pound was worth 1,200 roubles.

If the passengers on the *Marlborough* would have preferred Russian food, there is no indication of it in any of the memoirs. Indeed, Youssoupov recalled a daily timetable dominated by meals that were as English as they were welcome. 'After months of deprivation, everybody realised that they were hungry,' he wrote. 'Never had English cuisine seemed so delectable. Never had we so savoured white bread, which we'd forgotten the taste of. The three consecutive sittings imposed on the refugees were not enough to satisfy the ravenousness. Even between the allotted meal times we carried on eating...

'In the morning we were up early to attend the colours,

during which the band played English and Russian hymns. Then to the dining room where a copious breakfast awaited us. We returned to the bridge, already impatient to hear the gong which would announce lunch. A siesta, more or less prolonged, took us to the hour of tea. The three hours that separated us from dinner passed itself with visits from one cabin to another and in various games.'

In the early months after the Revolution, the Romanovs in the Crimea had existed almost exclusively on fruit and vegetables. The chef had apparently mastered the art of making Wienerschnitzel with cabbage and carrots. In May 1917, the revolutionary paper, *Izvestiya*, had reported approvingly: 'Goods and produce for the members of the former Dynasty are distributed by a rationing system, providing conditions equal to those for the general public, and none of the requests for extra food products are met. For example, Marie Feodorovna's [the Dowager's] request for three extra poods of sugar for jam-making was refused.'

The captives had all, at one point, been given ration cards for sugar. Signing her first one 'Marie', the Dowager was told it was insufficient. 'I have been signing "Marie" for fifty years, if it is not sufficient I can do without the sugar,' she retorted. The Crimean Regional Social Committee's sour conviction that the area around Yalta was infested with monarchists was borne out, during these early days, as locals, hearing of the Romanovs' rations, left pounds of sugar, bread and even cakes.

But the vagaries of the food provision worsened after the Bolshevik Revolution. Youssoupov later claimed that the family had to become accustomed to eating donkey for lunch and billy-goat for dinner. At one point they were having to make do with coffee made from roasted acorns, tea from hips and butter that looked like vaseline and tasted like petrol. As Prince Dmitri recalled: 'apart from pea soup, there were two different dishes; fried potatoes with onions and fried potatoes without...'

The mood of the captives would not have been lifted by unappetising food parcels received sporadically by the Dowager from her native Denmark. The parcels mostly contained tins of spaghetti, macaroni and meats, and manifestly failed to satisfy the Dowager, who complained to her son that she was hungry all the time.

Youssoupov, who was so relishing the pleasures of the table on the *Marlborough*, would dine in a velvet skull cap. When asked his reasons for this, the subject of Rasputin's murder would inevitably arise. As the ADC in Malta, Captain Ingham, later reported: 'I asked Prince Dolgorouky [the Dowager's equerry] afterwards why he wore this and he told me that the Prince had received head wounds at the time of the killing of Rasputin.'

While none of the sailors records details, Pridham mentions that Youssoupov spoke several times about his killing of Rasputin. The recollections would doubtless have gone down well with the officers. Perhaps it was on the *Marlborough* that Youssoupov developed the taste for entertaining audiences with tales of gory deeds, a habit that would dominate his social life in exile. In his memoir, Pridham's reference is perhaps overly proper and oblique: 'Although the Prince gave some of us an account of how he and his friends succeeded in their design I shall not repeat the story here, for it has been well told by him in his memoirs.'

While the *Marlborough* was anchored at Prinkipo, the Dowager was visited by little Sofka's maternal grandmother, Nadezhda Bobrinski, otherwise known as 'Granny Bob'.

There was a mixture of bravery and outlandish behaviour in the female line of Sofka's family. Sofka's mother had trained as a doctor, then won two George Crosses for bravery; but she also enjoyed smoking opium with Youssoupov. After the Second World War, Sofka herself would be given an award for saving the lives of Jews; but, in the end, she was better known for her louche lifestyle and, more controversially, her espousal of Communism.

Granny Bob's wild streak appeared to be confined to bravery. In her memoir, Sofka was full of admiration for her grandmother: 'She was organising a Red Cross Unit to join the White Armies fighting in the south near the Persian frontier. A year or so later came news of her death from typhoid. She had apparently refused to leave her post and went on caring for the dying and the wounded until she herself eventually succumbed.'

By the end of the day, Fothergill had betrayed himself as, at that point, no more than a partial fan of the Dowager. He breezily passed up an opportunity to dine with her, once one of the most coveted invitations in all of the Russias. As he told Punch: 'The Empress requests three officers to dine with her every night. I didn't feel like it myself so told three others to do it.'

The Dowager seems, however, to have been pleased with his choice. More importantly, she now insisted that she and the Captain had overcome their difficulties and were getting along famously. 'Captain Johnson and three officers joined us for meals. We are now already great friends with the Captain,' she wrote. She doubtless believed her own confident appraisal, but it is evident from her subsequent behaviour that she never quite lost her chariness towards him.

The Dowager, at any rate, looked forward to reaching Malta. She sent the briefest telegram to her sister: 'Just arrived here all well. Heartbreaking to leave beloved country. Delighted got your two dear letters and that from dear Waldemar. Thousand thanks. Staying here couple of days. Will give you news from Malta. Love to you all. Sister Dagmar.' The telegram makes no mention of her disappointment at the Grand Duke's party's failure, yet again, to disembark.

Day 7

SHIP'S LOG APRIL 13:
AT HALKI ISLAND
09.00 HELD HOLY COMMUNION SERVICE
HELD DIVINE SERVICE – HIH EMPRESS MARIE AND
ROYAL FAMILY ATTENDING.
15.30 HOISTED COLOURS
LANDED ARMED PARTY OF MARINES ON HALKI
ISLAND TO PROTECT LUGGAGE BEING LANDED FROM
HIBISCUS (REFUGEES' LUGGAGE)

The Captain had quite understood the importance of religion for the Romanovs. Eighty years later the Tsar, Tsarina and their five children were all canonised by the Orthodox Church. Though the Church's decision had a political element, it was also a tribute to the family's devotion. After the canonisation, their last days at Ekaterinburg came to be seen as a sort of road to Calvary, though doubters questioned the extent to which they had really been aware of their fate.

In any case, Johnson ensured that the ship's chaplain, the Rev Reginald Churchill, held a service for Palm Sunday on deck. Both Fothergill and Pridham mentioned the service, though Fothergill was, as usual, briefer: 'Rather a busy morning, dull sort of day – had church on the upper deck under the awning. The whole party attended.' Pridham wrote: 'At Halki, the Empress and twenty others attended church in the morning. The padre preached well and I think those who were able to follow it were greatly impressed.'

Halki was the second largest of the Prince's Islands. In the 1500s, it had provided a haven for an Elizabethan ambassador anxious to escape the bustle of Constantinople. Of more interest to the *Marlborough* passengers, however, would have been the island's 11th-century Greek Orthodox monastery.

The Dowager had a reputation as a flamboyant socialite with a vast collection of jewels, coquettish fans and a sable coat costing £12,000. She had brought a collection of jewels to the Crimea and, after the searches, had taken to hiding them in cocoa tins under rocks. The spots were marked with a dog's skull.

But she successfully combined her weakness for material wealth with a keen religious devotion. When she converted to Orthodoxy, she had not flinched from any of the strictures, even cursing the Lutheran faith and spitting three times. During her subsequent period at the helm of the Russian Court, all the fasts and Holy Days – taking up almost a third of the year – had been observed.

At her last meeting with her son, after his abdication, they attended church together at Mogilev, the military headquarters where the Tsar was based as head of the Army. For the first time in 304 years, the Imperial Family was not mentioned in the prayers. As the Dowager later watched the train carrying Tsar Nicholas away for the last time, she made the sign of the cross. That evening, in her diary of March 21st, 1917, she wrote: 'One of the most awful days in the life! When I was separated from my beloved Nicky!... an awful sorrowful parting! May God hold His hands over him...' When she herself returned to Kiev, there was no reception committee, no Cossack escort and the Imperial waiting room was closed.

In her early days in the Crimea, the Dowager had sat on her balcony deriving comfort from reading her old Danish family Bible. But, during a search, it was confiscated by a brazen guard, who snatched it out of her hand with an admonishment: 'This is an anti-revolutionary book and an old lady like you should know better than to poison her brains with such trash.'

It was said that, at the last minute before leaving Koreiz, she had insisted on praying again in a church. When she was told that they were all locked up, she had apparently said she must visit one, even if she had to knock down its doors with her bare hands.

The Dowager had a simple but robust faith, doubtless one of the factors in her belief that her son and his family survived. Unlike her daughter-in-law the Tsarina or, indeed, the Black Sisters, who dabbled in faith-healing and seances, she had no time for the more outlandish aspects of mysticism.

Now she found herself more than happy with the Rev Churchill's simple service: 'I got up early then we had a lovely service, the English priest preached so well about Palm Sunday, the sailors sang and then the musicians played our two hymns, which are so touching to hear again.'

The Dowager was recovering from her disappointment with the Dardanelles and beginning to relish aspects of life on board when she was visited by yet more victims of the Revolution: a Madame Tolstoy and her two children. Later, thoroughly out of temper again, she wrote: 'Those Bolshevik rascals had captured that poor little son and held him hidden for eleven days so the unhappy mother did not know where he was. Finally she received an anonymous suggestion to pay out a million roubles and then they would hand him over, those vile scoundrels, but the boy managed to flee without a payment, thank God.'

A few days later, Pridham alluded to the boy who, he said, was 'more or less tortured to say where his people could be found; he hadn't the faintest idea and could not have told them if he had wished'.

There were others on board beset by equally persistent voices of woe. No amount of games of patience could protect Papa Felix, or Prince Youssoupov (sen), from his. Pridham, noting his plight, was tentatively sympathetic: 'For the last year they (the Youssoupovs) have fed and housed 175 people, who had been hunted out by the Bolsheviks, in their own house in the Crimea. These poor wretches are now cast away on the world, goodness knows where, with in most cases no money... Every boat now brings letters for the Youssoupovs asking for assistance which it is not now in their power to give.'

Pridham only gradually learnt the details of what his passengers had been through. Such was his growing sympathy, and indeed anger, that he now became more expansive in his diary: 'In the afternoon I had a long yarn with Princess Obolensky, she was the first lady-in-waiting the Empress had on her arrival in Russia. She talked about the Tsar and the Revolution and Bolshevik raids last year.

'They all say the same thing about the Tsar and his interpretation of his Coronation vows being that he was solely responsible for the ruling of his people and unable to delegate authority to others. There were many tyrants amongst the nobility, tyrants as we should see them, but the Tsar was not one of these...'

The voluble Princess had then hastily reassured him that the *Marlborough* was, of course, free of these tyrants: 'The Empress Marie had herself selected those who should accompany her in HMS *Marlborough* and that was sufficient warranty.'

He raged against the Bolsheviks, though the specific raid he mentions was, strictly speaking, carried out by some 50 of Kerensky's Provisional Guards: 'The stories of the Bolshevik raids on the Royal estates in January last year are inconceivable. Apart from murder, torture, etc of everyone connected with the Imperial Families they could lay their hands on, their treatment of the Empress was disgusting.

'It was all done by sailors from Sevastopol. They say they were woken at 5.00am by finding sailors in their rooms. Some of these forced their way into the Empress's room, pulled her out of bed and made her stand while they ransacked everything on pretence of looking for counter-revolutionary documents. They insulted her in every way, smashed her icons and picture of the Tsar and his family and through it all she was standing bare-footed and in only the clothes she got out of bed in. After this they shut them all up in a little room for the remainder of the day and would allow them no clothes or food.'

It was later reported that, far from being cowed by the sailors, the stalwart Dowager complained continually. Indeed, at one point the exasperated men threatened to take 'the old hag' away with them. The Countess Yekaterina Kleinmichel, her lady-in-waiting, later wrote: 'Marie Feodorovna asked to be allowed to get up and dress in private, but this request was impudently refused. The soldiers withdrew for a moment, leaving an horrible old woman to watch her.'

The Dowager would not have been consoled by the Sevastopol Central Committee's subsequent boast that 'an horrible old woman' was a fully-fledged member of the Professional Women's Union. In a letter to Queen Olga of Greece, the Dowager complained that she was not even allowed to use the chamber pot. As the sailors left, the Dowager suffered a final insult. Her chauffeur declared himself a Communist and drove off in her motorcar.

During the raid, Xenia proved herself as stout-hearted as her mother. She left an account of the search: 'we were awoken by a frenzied banging on the door... A loud, foul voice screamed out "Open this door immediately! immediately!"' Undaunted, she challenged the sailor in charge, demanding to know if he were a Christian. If he was, she added, he should show more respect and remove his cap in front of the icons. He 'shamefacedly took it off.'

The sailors had been intending to intimidate her sons, the 16-year-old Dmitri and his 15-year-old brother Rostislav, who were at that point both in bed. But, as it turned out, the guard in charge of the boys fell into a drunken sleep, his gun propped between his legs. In the end the greatest disturbance the brothers suffered was the noise of a furious Red officer rousing and reprimanding the guard. When the officer spotted Dmitri's cadet uniform, he tore the Tsar's initials from the epaulettes and put them in his pocket. The boys were nonplussed as they were ordered to stay in bed for most of the morning, their hands above the sheets.

At Dulber the sailors harassed young Roman, who recalled: 'This person, who had a red band on his sleeve, ordered me to remain in bed while he searched my two rooms.' The sailors took Grand Duke Peter's hunting rifles and, more mysteriously, Militsa's gardening notebook. Roman added a sardonic comment: 'the notebook... contained the names of firms, Russian, French and German, where mother placed her orders. No doubt those addresses were of immense importance to those seeking the plans of counter-revolutionaries.' From Tchair, the sailors seized Nikolasha's diaries, letters and papers along with a fine collection of English shotguns.

Pridham's anger with the Bolsheviks is unlikely to have been quelled by tales of repentant, even weeping, revolutionaries. However, he described without further comment a moving exchange between the Dowager and one particular guard: 'All Russian soldiers used to wear a little cross round their necks and this has always been a most treasured symbol, the Bolsheviks abolished it at once. Shortly after the raid' [actually quite a long time after] 'and while they were still under guard, the Empress asked one of the soldiers who were on guard where his cross was, being alone she thought she might learn something of the ordinary peasant's feelings. After a first denial of all knowledge of it, he then very shamefacedly took it from his pocket and gave it to her, she then made him come near and she herself put it back in its old place round his neck... He wept like a child.'

Prince Roman witnessed a similar betrayal of loyalty. While being questioned during the search, Roman had started to play the piano with one finger. 'The sailor asked my name; I said I was the son of Grand Duke Peter who owned the castle and I started playing "God Save The Tsar".' He recalled how the sailor sighed deeply and murmured softly: 'The devil take all the deputies and send them to hell.'

Before the Revolution, the controversial Tsarina would insist: 'the peasants love us.' But, in the end, as far as Pridham was concerned, no amount of adulation could compensate for their shortcomings: 'The Russian peasant was lazy and had an amazing capacity for doing without.'

On board the *Marlborough*, the Romanovs may have tantalised themselves with these odd memories of simple devotion. But the troubling fact was that, for many of them, there remained no welcome anywhere.

Both Pridham and Fothergill seemed to take the continuing stalemate in their stride. As Pridham wrote: 'Nothing seems to be settled yet about where the two parties will go. The Empress has expressed a wish to see the C-in-C and Danish Minister tomorrow so perhaps we shall hear something definite then. Baron Staal has been ashore in Constantinople all day trying to find accommodation for the Grand Duke, but returned having found nothing.' Fothergill also wrote of nothing happening: 'Still no news, we are waiting till the Grand Duke can get some place to go to ashore.'

The Dowager, however, was becoming dissatisfied. She had expected the Grand Ducal party to disembark the day before. She wanted them off the ship. 'The Cockroaches no longer think about leaving us. *Soi disant* they have been looking for an opportunity to stay in Constantinople, but there are none to be had.'

While contemplating her own future, perhaps she should not have been so complacent. Clearly, despite the positive correspondence being carried on between the Palace and the Foreign Office, the problem of what would happen to the Dowager was being discussed on board the *Marlborough*. Somehow the 11-year-old Princess Sofka Dolgorouky got a whiff of difficulties regarding the Dowager and her prospects in England. She would have had no reason to make anything up. As she wrote: 'Although the British Navy had been sent to the rescue of Queen Alexandra's sister it had not been decided whether she was to come to England or not. One gathered that on some previous visit she had not made herself popular.'

The Dowager had been in England so frequently that she had almost come to regard it as a second home. In 1913 she had enjoyed a reunion at the Ritz Hotel in London with her youngest son, Grand Duke Michael, banished after an unpopular marriage. At the outset of the First World War, in 1914, she had been on a visit to London; Xenia and her husband Sandro had stayed at the Piccadilly Hotel and Felix and Irina at their smart Knightsbridge flat.

In fact, there was very little likelihood of the Foreign Office changing its tactic regarding the Dowager. Three months earlier, in January 1919, Sir Ronald Graham had written a private letter to Admiral Wemyss: 'There are not the same reasons against the Dowager Empress of Russia coming to this country as in the case of the Grand Dukes... but the Foreign Office wish to retain the right of being consulted before the journeys to England of any other prominent Russians as pre-facilitated by the Admiralty.' Wemyss himself had referred to the situation, in minutes: 'there can be no objection to the arrival of this unfortunate lady'.

At a lesser level, on the *Marlborough*, the 'unfortunate lady' continued to make strides with the British officers. Fothergill now found himself targeted: 'Sunday night... just returned from dining after sat next to the Grand Duchess Xenia (sister of the Tsar) she talked English very well, my neighbour on the other side had only a limited vocabulary.

'After dinner the Empress asked me to sit down by her and we were talking for a long time. It seemed so funny when she talked about her sister [Queen Alexandra] she told me she wanted to stay on in the ship and be taken to England but I don't think we can be spared.' Fothergill gave no intimation that he was unwilling to extend the Dowager's journey on the *Marlborough*.

Pridham recorded later, in his memoir, that dinner was as usual, but he couldn't resist the temptation to reflect, once more, upon the allure of the Dowager: 'There was no ceremony except at the moment when Her Majesty, a superb picture of stately grace, entered the dining cabin.'

It was at this point that he chose to compare the Dowager to her less popular daughter-in-law, the Tsarina. Before meeting the Romanovs, Pridham had not been particularly interested in events at the Russian Court. The negative impression he had of the Tsarina must, therefore, have reflected general British opinion. As he put it: 'I was constantly reminded of how greatly the character of the Empress Marie differed from that of the Empress Alexandra.

'Although of small stature, her [the Dowager's] bearing was so majestic that when she entered a room the eyes of everyone were riveted upon her... She possessed that invaluable gift of memory for faces and incidents connected with them, that seems inherent in Royalty.

'The Empress Alexandra, on the other hand, suffering from hysteria, was fanatically religious, proud, highly strung and unbending. As the years passed she became increasingly unresponsive to the demands of public opinion.'

Fothergill, meanwhile, did not allow his growing appreciation of his passengers to stop him proceeding with an account of the rest of the day's news: 'Just before dinner the Captain took one of the picket boats to call on the Turkish Commandant and ran her ashore, got her off this afternoon and hoisted her in, with a large hole in her, such is life!!'

Nor could he resist reports of further perfidies committed,

after dinner, by the ever more badly behaved French: 'Rather a panic after I got away as we got a report from the shore to say that drunken French sailors (protect us from our allies!!) were looting the refugees' luggage so we switched search lights on and landed some marines to guard the gear. The French are the limit, the Russians hate them now and I don't wonder. Well I must finish for today, rather wearing, I wonder how it is all going to end.'

Pridham elaborated: 'The French soldiers were all drunk and the Greek and Turkish inhabitants looked as if they might take it into their heads to help the French soldiers loot the baggage.' In his memoir, he gave a longer description: 'a British officer came on board to obtain assistance in guarding piles of baggage on the pier at Halki, which had been left there by the refugees while they sought lodging. He told us that many of the French soldiers, who were supposed to be in charge of the arrangements for receiving the refugees, were drunk and seemed likely to assist a band of local ruffians, collecting in the vicinity, in looting this baggage on the pier. He said that he had failed to find any officer in charge of the French soldiers. Perfidious Albion promptly landed a sufficiently large guard and all was well!'

The bad behaviour would have marked a rare moment of accord between the Greeks and French who, though they were meant to be allies, were at loggerheads in the Crimea. According to Pridham, the French were riled after Greek sailors tied a dummy to the yardarm of one of their ships – a wry reference to the French mutineers. A British battleship was eventually installed between the Greeks and French ships. Subsequent scrapping on the streets of Sevastopol was less easy to deal with.

The following day Pridham reported a successful resolution to the difficulties on the pier, the more gratifying for its British understatement: 'I hear that a certain amount of the refugees' luggage was stolen last night before our armed party got ashore, however a demonstration made by marching down one or two streets in the vicinity of the piers and posting sentries stopped any further attempts.'

Fothergill concludes his letter with: 'SUBHEAD: Monday... the Empress saw the C-in-C this morning and we are probably staying here a week and then most likely Malta.'

Day 8

SHIP'S LOG APRIL 14:
AT ANCHOR OFF HALKI
06.00 LANDED ARMED PARTY OF MARINES TO PROTECT
RUSSIAN REFUGEES 'LUGGAGE'
HANDS CLEANING SHIP AND PREPARING FOR PAINTING.
21.40 2 ABSENTEES RETURNED ON BOARD

Uncertainty was something the Dowager had learnt to live with. In the Crimea she had had to adapt to living under the various regimes. Under the Bolsheviks she would have been expected to embrace a different alphabet and a different calendar as her new rulers switched from Julian to Gregorian – 13 days ahead. The Bolsheviks then made a further decision to put the clocks forward two hours. In their last diaries, in July 1918, the captive Tsar and Tsarina attempted to retain some equilibrium by recording both old and new dates and times.

The Dowager would have found the clock change particularly aggravating. She had a despotic attitude to time; on one occasion Commander Turle's officer arrived at her estate to find the whole household dining an hour early simply because the Dowager's watch was fast.

Given her pernickety approach to plans and arrangements, the Dowager would have been gratified at this point in the *Marlborough* journey to learn that one of the most irksome of her uncertainties was finally going to be brought to an end. Her diary entry was jubilant: 'Now at long last it has been decided that the Dulbers will have another ship, which was a most agreeable piece of news. They themselves do not talk about this and say nothing.' She makes no reference to dashed hopes of the past. Clearly she felt, rightly as it turned out, that this time her wish had come true.

Nikolasha could hardly have failed to notice the Dowager's continuing hostility or her triumph at his impending departure. In recent years he had shaken off much of his trademark insensitivity. Well into the 'yellow leaf' period of his life, he had made every effort to forego the sword for the pen. He was embroiled in memoirs which the Soviet newspaper, *Izvestya*, admitted 'in the opinion of informed individuals are of great historical interest'. He was also writing a history of the reign of Tsar Nicholas II and finishing a challenging article: 'Who Is The Real Culprit of the World War?'

Indeed, so steeped had the Grand Duke become in his reflective life in the Crimea that he had refused to see anyone who might try to inveigle him back into action. As Prince Roman recalled: 'Uncle Nikolasha lived a cloistered life in his Tchair estate and refused to receive any visitors from the North, no matter who they were.' His dalliances with the sword were limited, like his brother's, to shooting birds on the seashore.

But if it was this cussed streak that kept him so stubbornly inactive in the Crimea, it was also the force behind his enduring loyalty to the Dowager. He was not about to let mixed messages deflect him from his duty. When the

Bolshevik Commandant at Dulber had handed the Romanovs back their guns to protect themselves, Nikolasha had spent the night standing guard at the Dowager's door. She, perhaps disdaining the fuss, had devoted herself to the card game bezique.

Now, on the *Marlborough*, Nikolasha was no less conscientious. On this morning, as on every other, he and the Dowager performed a ritual they had established on the first day. Nikolasha would approach the Dowager on deck, where she would already be installed on her deckchair, and bow and kiss her hand. As she dutifully extended a hand on this day, for the sixth time, thoughts of his imminent departure may have given her gesture an added piquancy.

The sailors, most of them oblivious of any underlying turmoil, found the ceremony extremely moving. Pridham was unequivocal in his admiration: 'With stately dignity he approached the Empress, who was already seated on deck, presented himself to her with an immaculate military salute, and then paid her courtly and graceful homage by bending low and kissing her hand. The spectacle of this immensely tall man in his striking Cossack costume and the stately little old lady – his Empress – was indeed touching. Whenever we were able, those of us who could find an excuse for being in the vicinity, made a point of watching this charming daily act of medieval chivalry.'

But if the sailors saw nothing beyond a harmonious tableau, the British authorities, curiously, were aware that the Dowager was anxious to separate herself from the Grand Duke's party. A telegram, sent on the same day as her jubilant diary entry, weighed up several possible scenarios for the future. The C in C Mediterranean, Constantinople, mentioning her desire for separation, suggested a highminded motive far removed from straightforward animosity. As he wrote to the Admiralty: 'Empress proposes to visit England and then to go to live in Denmark. Her immediate movements are complicated by the fact that she does not wish the two Grand Dukes and their party numbering 28 all told to accompany her to Malta, perhaps desiring to avoid embarrassing British Government.

'Grand Dukes are now asking Italian permission to reside in Italy with their families. Meanwhile as accommodation cannot be procured for Grand Dukes in Constantinople and as HMS *Marlborough* very crowded I hope to transfer them and their party to HMS *Lord Nelson* on Wedn. 16th April.'

In the course of this particular day, the Dowager had further triumphs. She succeeded in persuading the British Admiral Calthorpe to allow the *Marlborough* to remain anchored at Halki for a week – in order to be able to stay for Easter.

The officers reported the new development without further comment. As news spread that the ship would be anchored for a week, the passengers staying on board besieged Pridham with requests to gain access to their luggage. The weather had improved and many of them were running short of suitable clothes. Pridham vented his irritation, at the time, on the Russian servants. 'Fortunately I expected this and as far as was possible have made arrangements. Among other things I have organised a laundry for them in the Ward room bathroom. The chief difficulty is the Russian servants who are worse than useless, even when told to stand by their luggage for a few minutes they got tired of it and wandered away.' It was not until he wrote his memoir, years later, that he expressed sympathy for their plight.

He referred to the ship's delayed departure: 'I understand

now that the reason for the delay in our departure for Malta is that the Empress wishes to have a last chance of being with the remnant of her people for Easter. Easter is the biggest festival of the year in Russia. She wishes to arrange a special service for the refugees in Halki and will attend herself.' In fact, as it turned out, plans changed again and Easter was celebrated on the *Marlborough* at sea. The ship arrived at Malta on the afternoon of Easter Day.

Meanwhile, such time left to Pridham was spent organising trips off the ship for his restless passengers. He later wrote with some chagrin that everybody had enjoyed the trips ashore but he had been prevented from leaving the ship by 'a continual stream of people coming to see Her Majesty...'

The patriotism that bound the crew together was, at this point, given a fillip by yet more unseemly behaviour from the French. The affront, more of a lapse of taste, was noted by Pridham in his account of the day. Its victims, female members of the Romanov party, however, made no mention of it. 'The French are behaving in a disgusting manner. A case occurred this afternoon when some of our passengers were waiting for our boat to come in and fetch them off, they were sitting about ten yards away from the windows of a house in which were a lot of French officers, these beasts amused themselves by using their glasses to stare at the ladies. It doesn't really make it any worse, but the ladies in this case were all of them of Royal blood.'

With plans at least settled for the following week, Pridham reported an agreeable dinner: he was 'bidden to dine with the Empress at a most interesting dinner, sat between Princess Olga Orloff and Princess Dolgorouky and opposite Grand Duchess Xenia who was made to laugh I think for the first time since she arrived on board.'

Xenia's equable humour must have required some effort of will. She was grieving, in some way, for two brothers: a month before the murder of the Tsar and his family, her younger brother, Grand Duke Michael, had been shot in a forest in Siberia. While a question mark hung over all the deaths, she feared the worst. And though her daughter and five of her sons were now with her, she must have been worried about her eldest, Andrei, who was at large somewhere in Europe.

But she had proved her essential good nature while in captivity, even managing to befriend her Bolshevik guards. In a letter, written at the end of 1917, to her brother the Tsar, then in Siberia, she had written: 'Our guard consists of a mere fourteen men. Sometimes we chat with them when we meet (with the more pleasant ones!) and there are really some quite decent ones among them. They have allowed me to address them as "thou" and we have all come to the conclusion that this is much nicer and more egalitarian.'

In fact, her considerable charm had on occasion led her astray. Aside from her Englishman, Fane, Xenia had had several other lovers; so too had her husband Sandro. At one stage the complications were complete as Xenia elected to have an affair with Sandro's lover's husband. During their Crimean exile, relations had been particularly strained as she and Sandro found themselves obliged to share a bedroom. They must both have been relieved when Sandro decided to leave months earlier for Paris. There were rumours that Xenia's youngest son, Vassily, was in fact the son of the Dowager's equerry, Serge Dolgorouky. But Sofka's granddaughter, Sofka Zinovieff, now maintains no one took the rumours very seriously.

Day 9

SHIP'S LOG APRIL 15:
AT ANCHOR OFF HALKI
09.00 PAINTING SHIP
18.20 4 ABSENTEES RETURNED ON BOARD.

The last day with the Dulbers on board proved uneventful: one, as Pridham reported, 'of much coming and going'. 'Arrangements have now been made for the *Lord Nelson* to come here tomorrow morning and for us to transfer the Grand Ducal Party to her for passage to Genoa. This party consists of fourteen and their maids etc.'

Both Pridham and the Dowager mentioned a visit from White Army officers in a dilapidated old tug boat which drew up, unexpectedly, alongside the *Marlborough*. One of the officers told Pridham that they were too ill-dressed to come aboard but that they would like to have a glimpse of the Dowager. They explained that they had picked up the tug in Odessa and brought refugees to Constantinople.

Pridham was extremely impressed when the Dowager, far from being put off by the officers' soiled dress, climbed down a steep ladder to visit them. 'The Empress went down into the tug and spoke to them all as they were, some out of the engine room, and shook hands with them. Another day of much coming and going.'

The Dowager described the visit in her first entry of the day: 'Up early. Received General Schwartz who told us about the shameful conduct of the French in Odessa, who left the town without paying attention to his protests. I also saw his two very nice ADCs and young Alexeiev. The little steamer which brought them on board only had officers instead of sailors, only three were naval officers, the others infantry men. I went down to greet and talk with them, at first they didn't want to shake hands since they were so dirty. Everything seems so incredible.'

Years later, Prince Dmitri recalled trips ashore to Constantinople – including one to the stunning Hagia Sophia, although he seemed to remember little detail of this visit. Perhaps it was the fabled Romanov reticence. As Dmitri's nephew, Prince Rostislav, later said of his uncles: 'They spoke six languages but nobody ever said anything, so they were always referred to as being silent in six languages.'

For Dmitri, memories of Hagia Sophia were limited to the cheering vision of his elder sister in the throes of a cultural difficulty: 'On entering the building we were provided with special slippers which we were obliged to place over our shoes. Irina somehow managed to lose one of hers and completed the tour hopping through the building on one leg'.

The disagreeable Miss King found neither beauty nor joy in Constantinople, pronouncing it 'filthy'. But her charge, little Sofka, was less critical; she retained a powerfully sensual memory. As she wrote: 'It seemed a huge and colourful extension of a Tartar village, certainly unlike any idea of a town that I ever envisaged. The weather, however, was fairly hot and the flies and the smells somewhat overwhelming.'

One of the Russian refugees travelling on another ship, Elizabeth Zinovieff, was also disenchanted with Constantinople, plagued with memories of bedbugs: 'They dropped off the ceiling like paratroopers and we were so busy killing them that we did not sleep much.'

The Dowager, doubtless relishing the prospect of the Grand Duke's imminent departure, wrote a happy conclusion to her day's entry: 'Dinner as always, thereafter we went up on the deck in the loveliest moonlight.'

Day 10

SHIP'S LOG APRIL 16:
AT ANCHOR OFF HALKI
10.00 PAINTING SHIP...
13.00 GRAND DUKE NICHOLAS AND PARTY LEFT SHIP
FOR LORD NELSON. DRIFTED. TRANSPORTED LUGGAGE
16.00 LANDED FOOTBALL PARTY
18.20PM LIBERTY. MEN UNDER ARREST

The day was dominated by the departure of Grand Duke Nicholas and his party. While the crew were looking forward to regaining space on the ship, many had formed attachments to members of the party. These attachments would now be severed, in all likelihood, for ever.

There was a busy exchange of keepsakes. Wrote Pridham: 'Started getting the Grand Dukes' luggage up and away in a Drifter, something well over two hundred packages, most of them very heavy ones, the Grand Duke Nicholas had managed to bring a great deal of his silver (and possibly gold) plate. The *Lord Nelson* arrived during the forenoon and the Grand Dukes left after lunch.

'We gave the Grand Duke Nicholas a photograph of the

ship which he has asked us to autograph. Saw the Sword of Honour which was given him by the Tsar during the war for the deliverance of Galicia, a most magnificent thing, an old Damascus blade fitted with a solid gold hilt of exquisite design, covered with diamonds varying in size from that of a threepenny bit. It must be of fabulous worth. All those who left were very full of thanks, rather embarrassing.' Pridham added later that the sword was 'unobtrusively wrapped in a rather grimy piece of wash-leather'.

The jolly-looking Princess Marina, whose English was so good, had proven particularly popular. In his memoir, Pridham paid her an elaborate tribute: 'I was sorry to lose the help of the Princess Marina before my task was done. While it was I who should have produced for her a certificate of merit, such an acknowledgement was reversed, for she presented me with a charming little sketch she had painted of a typical Crimean scene, with cypress trees, and the upper part of a minaret thrusting up into the blue sky.'

Chief Petty Officer (Stoker) Sidney Arthur Webber evidently shared Pridham's disappointment at the departure of Princess Marina, with whom he seems to have struck up quite a friendship, calling her 'Princess Ice-a-Creama'. On departing, Princess Ice-a-Creama presented Webber with a necklace comprising three amethysts set in gold joined by two thin gold bars. She also gave him two bottles of scent.

The gregarious Princess Marina also gave Seaman Joseph Albiston, aged 24, a ladies' gun. According to his grandson, the gun was French-made and intended to be kept inside a muff. Albiston, whose job before enlisting had been replacing bobbins in a cotton mill, had clearly made the most of his time with the Princess. On his service record Albiston's complexion was described as 'fresh'; 'He was a very good-looking man' as his grandson recalls.

The Dowager made the briefest mention of Nikolasha's departure. It was evidently a case of least said soonest mended: the 'cockroaches' no longer warranted attention. 'It was our last luncheon with the Dulbers, who left us at long last with their huge entourage in order to travel to Italy on board the *Lord Nelson* with Admiral Seymour.'

Fothergill covered Nikolasha's departure equally briefly in his diary: 'Grand Duke's party left for *Lord Nelson* at 1.20. guard and band. Peter [Grand Duke Peter] was very generous with thanks... Landed a marine picket. Picked up Dibble's [his sister Violet] "Turkish Delight".'

It is unclear who little Sofka missed most after the Dulbers' departure, particularly as none of the children left, but she recalled being unsettled. As she recounted in her memoir: 'At last we steamed off. The ship seemed enormous and there was nothing to do. I scrounged whatever books were to be found and played deck games with Vassily...' Deck games included quoits, dancing on the quarterdeck and teasing two of the dogs on board: Sofka's Pupsik – spelt by Miss King 'Poupsick' – and Xenia's Toby (the puppy, incidentally, of Pupsik.)

While Sofka remembered being bored, her companion Vassily's memories of the *Marlborough* were almost exclusively of intense enjoyment. He described his voyage to a friend, Albert Bartridge, who now recalls: 'Vassily said the children had the free run of the ship; the parents and carers were too preoccupied to worry about them.' The only sour note for Vassily was the disappearance of his pet canary, released through a window by one of his brothers.

Birds were a feature of the young Princes' lives; Dmitri recalled regular visits, as a child, to the HIMS *Aurora*, its main

attraction being a parrot which swore. He also had fond recollections of a pet cockatoo that was kept in a sewing room
next to his parents' bedroom: the noise of the machines would
drown the squawks of this equally foul-mouthed bird.

Marine Phillips described the two young playmates,
Sofka and Vassily, in a letter written to the BBC in 1971, a year
before he died: 'There were two children, a boy and a girl.
They would wander over the ship and show interest in the
guns etc...' One peculiarity of the pair's relationship is that,
when Sofka later wrote her memoir, she described Vassily as
'a couple of years my senior'. In fact, they were the same age,
11. Given children's preoccupation with their ages, it seems
unlikely that they had not discussed how old they were.
Perhaps Sofka's memory let her down. Or perhaps Vassily
added on a year or two; as the baby of a large family, he would
have relished some unaccustomed seniority.

The officers enjoyed chatting with the children on board.
Pridham had particularly fond memories of them: 'Prince
Vassily soon became a favourite throughout the ship; sailors
always love eager and inquiring children, this one was just the
type of lively youngster that appealed to them. Prince Dmitri
was full of enthusiasm for all things naval, indeed he seemed
to possess as complete a knowledge of British warships as I
had myself.'

The young Princes may have been cowed by the crew, or
lost in admiration. For whatever reason, they appear to have
been on best behaviour: the British officers had nothing but
praise for them. By the time they reached Malta, however,
after two weeks on the ship, their good behaviour quotient
seemed to have run out. The beleaguered English ADC later
reported that the boys tickled butlers' legs, tipped rifles out of
soldiers' arms and threw bread rolls at each other.

On the *Marlborough*, the Captain had taken pains over the wellbeing of the five youngest children. These under-sixes included Youssoupov's daughter Irina, aged five, Grand Duke Peter's granddaughter, also Irina, aged one, and Sofka's cousin, Olga Dolgorouky, four. He had arranged for an area of the deck to be put aside, with chairs for nannies and a rug for the children. The sailors were soon as much taken with these smallest passengers as they had been with the Princes and would frequently stop to play with them.

At the heart of this English-speaking enclave were the two principal nannies: Xenia's Miss Coster and the Youssoupovs' Miss Zillah Henton, 'Henty'. The pair would have been joined by a Miss Turk, about whom little is known and, finally, the forthright Miss King. While Miss King was not popular either with her charge or with Pridham, there is no evidence that she did not get along with the other nannies. They were, after all, fellow Englishwomen and proud of it. Indeed, the doughty Henty had at one point refused to wear a Bolshevik red rag, declaring herself too patriotic to wear a colour of revolution.

Though Miss Coster was frequently spotted chatting to the sailors, Miss Henton was more reticent. Nana Coster clearly had the edge over the 52-year-old Henty in terms of personal attractions. She retained a fine embonpoint, and years later Dmitri still recalled his nanny's 'big bosoms'. He recounted an excruciating memory of the Tsarevich Alexis once asking her: 'Why don't you place your coffee cup there?'

But Miss Coster had not been so lucky with her teeth which had, by then, all fallen out. Prince Dmitri later confessed that he had always been alarmed by his Nana's false teeth, which she placed in a glass of water by her bed every night: 'From the age of four I had a recurring nightmare in which Nana's

Sofka Dolgorouky, second from right, with Olga, her cousin, right. Nadezhda is on the left with her baby Irina, and Princess Irina Youssoupov and her daughter Irina are in the middle

The two baby Irinas, with a companion

false teeth were chasing me around the house.'

The Grantham-born Miss Henton was a sturdy character, full of northern grit. Shortly after the Revolution, while in the Crimea, she had confronted a crowd of revolutionaries who appeared in the drive of Ai-Todor. Henty had stood on the balcony, carrying baby Irina, while the Princes' Swiss tutor cunningly congratulated the crowd, before singing the praises of republican Switzerland. Reports differ on the tenor of the situation. Prince Dmitri, then 16, who had also been on the balcony, later saw it as the villagers naively wishing to celebrate the Revolution. 'Wearing red ribbons on their coats they marched happily up the drive, singing and smiling all the way. They gathered in the courtyard in front of the house and sang "The Red Flag". It obviously never occurred to them that they were congratulating the wrong people.'

Sofka Dolgorouky and Vassily

Years later, in 1984, Vassily's memory echoed Dmitri's: 'They congratulated us on the Revolution, the new Emperor and liberty... They didn't know what they were talking about.'

But whatever the extent of danger regarding this early demonstration, Miss Henton showed her mettle over the next couple of years. She bore witness to the brutality of the revolutionaries. In an interview with an English newspaper in the 1930s, she described revolutionaries shooting three members of the estate's 'outside staff' in cold blood: one was shot in the back as he tried to crawl beneath the floor of a granary.

She had been under no illusions about her own vulnerability; she spoke of all-night vigils, sitting beside little Irina's cot, a packed suitcase at her feet. She later told her family of one mysterious night when her master, Youssoupov, had tapped her on the shoulder and picked up Irina while she grabbed the suitcase; the pair had walked what felt like miles to a waiting car, then driven to safety.

It was Miss Henton who agreed to defy the guards when the Romanovs were incarcerated at Dulber and communication between the estates was forbidden. The only captives whose movements were not restricted were the doctor and little Irina. Miss Henton readily tied notes to the toddler's clothes, then watched her as she wobbled blithely between Koreiz and Dulber. As Youssoupov recalled: 'Her nurse took her to the gates of the park [at Dulber] and the child entered it alone, with our letters pinned inside her coat. The answers reached us in the same way. Our little messenger never let us down.' Youssoupov added that, without Miss Henton and Irina, the family were reduced to shouting over the walls for their dogs and hoping that one of the young Princes would appear.

Having successfully disembarked the Grand Ducal party and their luggage, Pridham thoroughly enjoyed the rest of his day. He derived a quiet satisfaction from completing uncomplicated tasks in the company of his favourite helpmate, Grand Duchess Xenia. Perhaps he was aware of the relief felt, in important quarters, at the final departure of the Dulbers. 'I spent the afternoon with the Grand Duchess

Xenia, re-arranging the cabins, bringing the older people up to the nicer ones and arranging more fresh air for the babies. A few more people are coming in the place of those who have left so there will still be no room to spare but it will be a little more comfortable.'

As regards the *Marlborough*'s plans, he felt that, with the British authorities' decision now to evacuate Russian refugees from Halki, the Dowager would have no reason to delay her departure for Malta: 'I think we shall leave for Malta on Friday evening so as to get in early Monday morning.'

There was only one small fly in the ointment: 'The Grand Duchess has asked me to get her some shoes for two of the refugees, I shall be able to, of course, but hope we shall not become a general supply ship for this kind of thing; it will be difficult to draw the line, so I shall ask her to take them from me as a gift to the Russian refugees, then she will see that an indiscriminate supply of government stores is unlikely.'

The Dowager reverted to fresh concerns about the behaviour of the French: 'After lunch I also received Metropolit Platon whom the French had chased away from Odessa! They are simply behaving awfully towards the poor refugees and all the Russians who are unlucky enough to be on their ships, do not even permit them to go ashore here... Then the Russian priest Nikolai arrived from Yalta and I went to Confession before going to Communion tomorrow.'

With the arrival of good weather later in the day, the Dowager's spirits lifted: 'Lovely weather warm and calm so that we spent the evening up on the deck.'

Pridham was also cheered: 'The weather has at last turned very hot, for some days past it has been quite cold, but now there is no wind at all and a blazing sun, "full white" weather but we are still in all blue.'

161

Day 11

Ship's log Thursday, April 17:
at anchor off Halki
07.00 embarking refugees luggage
09.00 divisions prayers   diving party
10.00 rest hands painting ship
hosted boats. prepared for sea

First thing in the morning, Fothergill recorded briefly: '*Lord Nelson* sailed at 7.00am with Grand Duke...'

The Dowager, apparently more absorbed in her account of Holy Communion, again barely mentioned the departure: 'We saw *Lord Nelson* weigh anchor and sail off to Genoa in the loveliest weather with all the Dulbers...'

The long-awaited departure of the Dulbers gave the Dowager a renewed zest for life. For the Dulbers, the effect of the separation was exactly the opposite. They were, by all accounts, sadder on this second leg of their journey than they had been on the *Marlborough*. It may have been that, away from the scrutinising eye of their Empress Dowager, they felt able to indulge their sorrow.

Years later, in the 1970s, a taped interview was given by

one of the sailors on the *Lord Nelson*: 'They [the Dulbers] was very as you might say well they'd suffered a disaster and you could see the effect of it at the time... They was full of tears and mourning, bereavement and they was a saddened party. There was no joy or no smiles, so we was under the impression that they'd, owing to the journey they'd had to make to be rescued, they must have suffered.'

It is curious that the Dowager gave so little outward indication of her suffering on the *Marlborough*. She refused to believe that either of her sons had been killed. It would be a full five years before the death of her younger son, Michael, was established, and she was long dead by the time the remains of the Tsar were found. She had, however, been all too aware of the terrible effects of the Revolution, not least the deaths of nearly ten Romanov cousins within the last year.

But Pridham had little time to contemplate the mood of his remaining passengers. He was now preoccupied with the evacuation of the Russian refugees from Halki; a situation lent more urgency by the paucity of the refugees' accommodation. It was 'awful, no furniture, the houses crawling with the worst kinds of beastliness...' he reported cryptically.

He wrote: 'The evacuation of all those who had been brought to Halki in British ships took place today. We had large parties of men ashore helping the re-embarkation of the refugees who are being taken to the *Bermuda* at Constantinople for passage to Malta. They are very pleased at being definitely placed under our protection and removed from that of the French.'

Fothergill makes a brief allusion to the tasks in his barely decipherable diary: 'Fine day – landed a large working party (100) to shift refugees' gear... Tried to dig out gear for GD...' GD here presumably means Grand Duchess.

While the refugees were being tended to, the younger *Marlborough* passengers were taken by some of the officers to the island. They relished speaking to some fellow countrymen. Though the Russians transported from Yalta had been evacuated, many more remained. Fothergill, who was among the party, mentioned a long-awaited swim in his brief diary entry: 'very hot day... in another picnic party landed on island, quite good fun, being hot, bathed for first time for I don't know how long.'

In his memoir, Prince Dmitri was more expansive, referring to a 'picnic arranged by some of the officers of our ship and we spent a delightful afternoon in the sun on Halki island.' Pridham mentioned the expedition, though he had been unable to go himself: 'The idea proved popular and it was not only the youngsters who spent a very pleasant afternoon in the delightful surroundings of a small cove well away from dwellings.'

The Dowager's afternoon on the *Marlborough* was spent more sombrely. She was visited by yet another woman who had suffered terribly in the Revolution. It is impossible to know how bruised the Dowager was by these visits. However, it is clear from her diary that, by the end of each day, she had sufficiently recovered to focus on other, less urgent matters.

Pridham gave a detailed description of her visitor in his diary: 'A lady in deep mourning came on board to see the Empress in the afternoon, I hear that less than six weeks ago she was sitting having tea with her husband in their house in the Crimea, when suddenly about half a dozen masked men burst in, called her husband in the hall and there shot him dead in front of his wife. It is this kind of thing which has been going on indiscriminately all over Russia for the last 15 months. None knew when it would be their turn, no wonder they are nervous wrecks now...'

His prediction that the *Marlborough* would leave for Malta on Friday was borne out: 'In the afternoon the C in C came on board and it was decided that we should leave for Malta tomorrow morning.'

The Imperial party of picnickers; below, landing on Halki

Day 12

SHIP'S LOG APRIL 18TH (GOOD FRIDAY):
AT SEA
09.20 DIVISIONS PRAYERS
PASSING THROUGH DARDANELLES

Fothergill gave a brief account of the day of departure from Halki in his diary: 'Off to Malta... prayers and hymns on upper deck... passing through the Dardanelles... Blowing and raining rather a dirty night.'

The Dowager's day began badly but improved; her detailed descriptions of the mild ups and downs give every indication, once again, that she was living in the moment: 'We got under way at 5.30 and I woke up from the dreadful noise. We spent the day on the deck to see the islands and so much beauty. After lunch I went with Lolo Dolgorouky to the Captain's upper cabin and from there he invited us right up to the bridge so that we could see the way out of the Dardanelles which was very interesting. We saw lots of shipwrecks on both shores, the results of war.'

Pridham was curiously unenthusiastic about the Dowager's venture onto the bridge; perhaps this was to do

166

with the idea's originating from the Captain: 'The Empress insisted on going up to the Bridge while we were passing through the interesting part of the Dardanelles, it is a long way up for an old lady like her.'

He added in his memoir that the sight of the Dardanelles brought back memories of the unsuccessful campaign in 1915. He mused wordily: 'It stirred the memory of us, both Russian and British, to regrets. Could not that magnificently conceived but alas ill-conducted and supported, outflanking movement against our common enemy have shortened the war and those fearful lists of casualties in France? Could it not have prevented the collapse of Russia, our ally, and the Revolution, and have rendered this sad journey inconceivable?'

Perhaps it was lucky that the Dowager was finally driven off the bridge by the weather. As she wrote: 'Unfortunately a sudden hard wind blew up which was intolerable. Then we all had tea together and I slept a little after that. After dinner we stayed down below as it was both raining and windy. I played patience with Zenaide [Felix Youssoupov's mother] and Aprak [the Dowager's lady-in-waiting, Princess Obolensky] till we went to bed.'

Pridham reported: 'Weather not too good after we cleared the Cape Helles, had to go round and shut up everything in case it got bad during the night, I had to perform this myself as a good many of them were in process of retiring for the night.'

Along with Fothergill, Prince Dmitri mentions a 'special midnight Good Friday service which ended with the traditional Russian response: "*Christos voskresi*", Christ is risen.'

Day 13

SHIP'S LOG APRIL 19:
AT SEA
07.00 SIGHTED LORD NELSON
12.40 PUT CLOCKS BACK 30 MINUTES

Fothergill's diary: 'rain squall... rather trying wind going down gradually. Clocks put back half an hour... got my hair cut.'

This was another poor day for the Dowager. Aside from having to contend with wind and squalls, she found herself confronting yet another obstacle to her wishes. The point at issue was whether the remaining Romanovs would have to transfer ships at Malta from the *Marlborough* to the *Lord Nelson*. The *Lord Nelson* would, in theory, be more comfortable, as it had been adapted to take passengers. But, as she had already intimated, the Dowager wished to be taken all the way to England on the *Marlborough*.

So exercised was she that she barely commented upon another sighting, that morning, of the *Lord Nelson* carrying away the dreaded Dulbers, or a spirited exchange of naval signals between the ships: 'I slept till 8 o'clock. The wind continues. I received a telegram from beloved Alix. It was only after lunch that I went up onto the deck, as there was a strong wind. Zina Mengden and her two nephews did not appear at all, they felt poorly even though there is hardly any noticeable sea. Just a pity that it rains from time to time, the waves are big and sometimes cover the whole deck... This morning we sailed past *Lord Nelson* which was moving so slowly that we soon lost sight of her.

'All the officers hope that their ship, the *"Marlb"*, will be permitted to bring us all the way to England, but unfortunately the Admiral has received orders from Malta that the *"Marl"* has to be sent back to the Black Sea and we will then have to go onboard *Lord Nelson* instead which is a dreadful pity.'

The Dowager's whims had an unattractive way of growing into obsessions. But they may have been born less of entitlement than despair. After two years of torment, the Dowager was locked in a never-ending battle with the last straw.

Pridham reported in his diary: 'Passed the *Lord Nelson* after breakfast, she is going straight to Genoa. There was an interchange of signals between the younger members. Weather not improving, the sea got up a little after rounding the South of Greece, some of my charges are not feeling very well.

'The Empress now expresses a great desire to go on to England in the *Marlborough*, instead of waiting at Malta. I am afraid it is not very likely as the C in C has already said that the ship is required in the Black Sea as soon as possible. However if the King were asked, no doubt arrangements would be made. Personally I should prefer to finish the job properly now we have got so far, also there would be a possible chance of putting in a week-end while there.

'They all want us to take them home so apparently they are

as comfortable as they hope to be.'

He described as an afterthought a welcome, if late, breakthrough in relations. A full 12 days after boarding the *Marlborough*, Felix Youssoupov's wife Irina was opening up: 'Princess Youssoupov has at last been induced to talk, she speaks English very well indeed.'

Pridham mentioned, finally, a midnight service at which the party sang their Easter hymn. Acting as server was 'Robbie' Roberts, later so convinced that none of the Romanovs believed the Tsar and his family had been shot. Roberts was also in charge of the practical arrangements, and had been responsible for setting up the ship's portable organ and altar.

Day 14

SHIP'S LOG APRIL 20 (EASTER SUNDAY):
AT MALTA
00.45 PUT CLOCKS BACK 30 MINUTES
03.10 SIGHTED LAND
06.55 FIELD MARSHALL LORD METHUEN
(GOVERNOR) VISITED EMPRESS
10.00 DIVISIONS PRAYERS HOLY COMMUNION SERVICE

The dawning of Easter Day 1919 on the *Marlborough* found the Dowager doleful: 'Easter Sunday. I couldn't sleep any longer as I had cramps in my leg and had to get out of bed. I was however up early but was not in the Easter spirit.'

Perhaps she dwelt on Easters long past. In the days of pre-revolutionary Russia, her son had traditionally embraced 1,600 grateful subject before giving eggs to them. Indeed he complained once that his cheeks would get 'terribly sore'. The Dowager, meanwhile, would distribute gold and enamel eggs to the officers of all her regiments.

An integral part of the celebration, since 1885, had been the lavish eggs containing 'surprises', delivered to the Dowager by the Imperial jeweller, Carl Fabergé. 'Your

171

Majesty will be pleased,' he would pronounce enigmatically. The surprises would include anything from a whimsical singing bird to a model of the newly opened Trans-Siberian railway.

The Dowager may have been mindful of the last Fabergé egg given to her, in 1916, the 'Cross of St George'. As its surprise, this egg contained miniature portraits of her son and grandson Alexis. It was now stowed below, in the hold of the *Marlborough*.

By Easter of the following year, 1917, the Tsar and his family had been placed under house arrest at Tsarskoye Selo and Fabergé had been refused admittance. He had remonstrated with the Provisional Leader, Alexander Kerensky, asking him to give the Tsar an invoice for 125,000 roubles, addressed, chillingly, to Nicholas Romanov.

By Easter 1918, the Bolsheviks had taken power and all the Romanovs were in terrible jeopardy. The Tsar and his family, now in Siberia, busily painted hens' eggs for Easter: within three months they would all be dead.

Their cousins in the Crimea, at that point all incarcerated at Dulber, also faced death. Prince Dmitri described their predicament in a letter to Mr Stewart, who would once again have taken issue with some of his pupil's English: 'then we went to Dulber there we lived like prisoners they did not let us out. Three times they wanted to kill us we had a projector alumenate the sea that no comes from there. A weak we did not undress we were all prepared to fight till the end the big ones had rifles.'

Despite the situation, elaborate preparations went ahead for Easter. Roman remembered curds, eggs and almonds being assembled, as usual, for the Easter meal. His father had converted one of the rooms into a chapel; he had invited a priest from the Tsar's palace of Livadia to officiate. There was only space for the Dowager, Grand Duke Peter and Militsa, Nikolasha and Anastasia in the room; the choir was obliged to stand by the door. Xenia's husband recalled: 'We made our peace with God in the chapel convinced that we would not live to see another Easter.'

It had been on the eve of Easter Day that the Crimean captives were told that the Germans had arrived and within an hour they would be free. Prince Vassily described that moment prosaically in an interview in 1984: 'He [the Bolshevik guard] sat on the telephone keeping them [the more aggressive faction of Bolsheviks] sort of talking instead of coming and killing us. But nothing happened because three Germans on horseback came into Yalta and the Bolsheviks disappeared.'

If the Romanovs' bitterness towards their German rescuers had been understandable, it had not been sustainable. The former prisoners had soon found themselves casting off their dog-in-the-manger constraints. A curious peace had followed the 'rescue', during which central preoccupations were, once again, poker, bridge and tennis tournaments. Dmitri recalled tennis balls being at a premium and racquets having to be restrung. To Mr Stewart, he had written: 'Here is a club at Michore teniss, Rostislav and I play like champions we also play at home. We have no teniss balls if you send us some, next ocassion I will write again.' Vassily, in the interview in 1984, added: 'Actually I was the freest of them all. I drove my friends around the estate without the groom.'

The Dowager described her relief to her sister: 'Otherwise we are all well, thank God, & move about in freedom, which is already a great happiness & a wonderful feeling after our long imprisonment.' Dmitri had repaired once again to his cooking chalet. The chalet had been created for him after he had seen the Tsar's daughters cooking vegetable pies at Peter-hof. 'It was this place which inspired me to build my own little house in fhe Crimea where I used to cook for invited guests.'

However, there had remained the odd reminder of their precarious position; on one of the boys' frequent trips to Yalta, their carriage had been shot at four times from the mountains. The shots had hit a rock on the side of the road. Dmitri wrote: 'although outwardly things seemed to have re-turned to normal we were still living in uncertain times.'

❧

For the Romanovs on board the *Marlborough*, Easter 1919 could obviously not match the grandeur of pre-revolutionary festivities. Nor could any celebration have quite the doom-laden resonance of their more recent Easters in the Crimea.

But Pridham was determined that Easter 1919 would be, at the very least, memorable. He was excited, that evening, as he recounted his painstaking preparations: 'Last night I got Schwerdt to paint a picture of the ship on hard boiled eggs for each of the five children, he did them excellently and they were a great success this morning. The babies were pleased and the grown ups pathetically touched. It is extraordinary how they appreciate a little thing like that – the reason why we are all in love with them, from the Empress down to the one-year-old baby.'

Pridham had spoken to Prince Orloff, whose English idi-om had so captivated the officers, about the various Russian Easter traditions. 'We also prepared Easter Eggs for the grown ups' breakfast, it is their custom to have coloured hard boiled eggs on the table. I'm not quite sure whether they eat them. I happened to discover this custom from a casual conversation and produced it as a surprise. The children's eggs had their initials painted on them in Russian characters and the letters XB which stand for: "Christ is risen". Orloff coached us in these details. We intended to tie each egg up in red tape, failing ribbon, but there was none on the ship!!'

Prince Dmitri, at any rate, was impressed. Years later he recalled: 'At breakfast on Easter Day we found eggs with the mark XB, together with our initials, painted on the shells in the Russian manner. These had been painted by the crew.'

While she put on an appreciative face for Pridham, the Dowager failed to regain her spirits: 'There was a service at 11 o'clock, the priest delivered a sermon but unfortunately without singing, but it was so pleasant to have at least something.'

Pridham was impressed by the importance of Easter to the Russians and dwelt further on the various rituals in his diary: 'During the day it is their custom to greet one another with three kisses and congratulations. The children have to go to the Empress and their mothers with a white flower first thing in the morning and offer their congratulations. Easter eggs are a great feature of the day, these are usually little gold and enamel ornaments, many of them very valuable. The ladies all wear strings of them, some being really magnificent.'

He was overwhelmed when he received several eggs, including two which he believed to be Fabergé, from the Dowager and Xenia. Particularly precious would have been the Dowager's egg, dated 1917 and originally intended for the officers of her regiments. He wrote in his diary that evening: 'The Empress used to present one to each officer of the regiments of which she is C-in-C. She gave me one of these, a pearl mounted in platinum with a tiny enamelled Russian flag on one side. I was also given two pretty ones for my own babies from the babies here. Various others were given me during the day, I have a regular collection of them.'

Later, in a foreword, Pridham gave a more formal account: 'For that year her [the Dowager's] Easter egg was a pearl carrying a minute platinum and enamel Russian ensign and the figure 1917, and was the last of such trinkets made for the Imperial Family by the famous jeweller Fabergé. I was the greatly privileged recipient from Her Majesty of one of these pearl Easter eggs, and from the Grand Duchess Xenia a very pretty gold and ruby one, also Fabergé.' In fact, the eggs turned out not to be by Fabergé. How Pridham got the impression they were remains a mystery. He was not given to fanciful thinking. It could be that one of the servants misinformed him. The Dowager was trying to glean favours from him, but she would surely not have resorted to exaggerating the eggs' provenance?

Perhaps buoyed up by the thoughtfulness of the officers as much as an improvement in the weather, the Dowager now felt ready to approach Pridham concerning her new campaign. She made no reference to their discussion in her diary; the subject needed to be handled with circumspection. She wrote simply: 'After lunch we sat upstairs, it was lovely clear weather but a strong wind, the sea was a lovely blue.'

But Pridham, while giving a nod to the weather, could not resist recording the details of such a gratifyingly intimate discussion: 'During the afternoon the Empress tackled me on the subject of the ship taking her to England instead of waiting at Malta for the *Lord Nelson* which is the present arrangement; she said she was pretending not to know anything about that. Of course I told her that we should much prefer to do so. She then showed me a draft of a telegram to the King she had written out, in which she said all sorts of nice things about us and urged that she should be allowed to complete the journey in the *Marlborough*.

'At any rate we know that we have pleased her, she is so tremendously keen on going on to England with us.' Later, in his memoir, he did acknowledge that, besides being smitten with the *Marlborough*, she had other reasons for not wanting to disembark: '...she particularly disliked the idea of disembarking at Malta and having to meet a great many new people while waiting for the *Lord Nelson* to arrive from Genoa.'

He continued in his diary: 'She is afraid the telegram will not have the desired effect, I endeavoured to assure her that if the King knew her wishes and expressed his wish, the necessary order would, of course, be given. It is quite funny, I am in the middle of a great conspiracy, she is feeling her way to tackling the Captain on the subject and is quite frightened of him.'

How well disposed King George V was feeling towards his aunt at that precise moment is not known. Having withdrawn his offer of exile to the Tsar, he had set about putting his unfortunate cousin to the back of his mind. Three days before the murder of the Tsar and his family, on July 17th, 1918, he had been attending a cricket match at Lord's.

But his mother had not allowed him to be so cavalier regarding her sister. From the beginning of the troubles, she had insisted he badger the British Ambassador Sir George Buchanan for news of the Dowager. Buchanan had attempted to reassure the King that he was using his influence with the Provisional Government to guarantee protection for her. But he had not seemed sympathetic to the Dowager's plight, particularly with regard to her diet, pointing out that Russia was suffering generally from food shortages. 'Her Majesty may not have been able to obtain some of the articles of food to which she is accustomed.' By September 1917, the Provisional Government had agreed to allow the Dowager Empress and select relatives to leave Russia for Great Britain. But no action was taken and a month later the Bolsheviks were in power.

It was a mark of the Dowager's confidence in the outcome of her campaign that she was able, that afternoon, to focus on the Captain's navigational skills: 'At 4.30 one could already see Malta in the distance. Immediately after tea we all went up to the bridge despite the strong wind to see the approach to Malta. I was all on my own up there and admired Captain Johnson's composure and firmness because it must indeed be incredibly difficult to sail that enormous ship into the narrow entrance to the harbour, which was crammed full of ships.

'We turned completely round among them, quite brilliant and were only tied on to two buoys, without anchoring. Unfortunately, it was not at all hot; thankfully the sun shone as we sailed in on the dot of 6.00. Immediately thereafter, Lord and Lady Methuen came on board together with the Admiral to welcome us. Lord Methuen had been wounded in the Boer War and has a stiff leg. They both seem to be charming people.'

According to Pridham, the Dowager was slightly evasive when Methuen began discussing her future plans. She was reluctant to commit herself when he told her that the San Antonio Palace had been prepared for her: 'The Empress, feeling that she was being hustled ashore from the *Marlborough* before the King could reply to her cablegram, demurred. However, the Governor told her that he was carrying out his instructions from England and that the *Lord Nelson* would be arriving shortly to take her to England. In the end the Empress agreed to disembark the following day.'

The Romanovs' last night on board the *Marlborough* was

suffused with a poignant conviviality. Youssoupov contributed to the festive atmosphere, bringing out his guitar for the last time on board. 'That was our last dinner with the dear Captain and our pleasant company,' the Dowager wrote, 'which hurts me to leave. We stayed down below as it was too cold upstairs. Felix sang most beautifully to his guitar while the rest of us played patience and listened.'

Once again she makes no mention of some vigorous, covert attempts at string pulling; but Pridham reports excitedly: 'During the evening I was given two telegrams, one for the King and the other for Queen Alexandra, with a request that I should get them sent as soon as possible. I got DAQMG – a Naval official – who came on board with the Governor, to deal with them and get a line cleared; they guaranteed to get them through to London in five hours. These telegrams were copies of the one the Empress showed me in the afternoon.'

The telegrams paid tribute to the *Marlborough*, speaking of the Dowager's gratitude for the 'hospitality and remarkable kindness from everybody here on board'. As Pridham recalled in the foreword to his memoir, he was specially requested to issue the two telegrams secretly, without telling the Captain.

Fothergill, excluded from this particular loop, recorded an uneventful day in his diary: 'blowing a little... had communion service... chaplain came over after supper... raining hard and rather beastly.' He continued in a letter to Punch: 'Arrived at Malta... about 5.00pm. The Governor Lord Methuen came on board to see the Empress.'

Day 15

SHIP'S LOG APRIL 21 (EASTER MONDAY):
AT MALTA
03.30 PUT CLOCKS BACK 20 MINUTES
04.30 PUT CLOCKS BACK 20 MINUTES
09.00 HIH EMPRESS MARIE OF RUSSIA AND ROYAL
FAMILY LEFT SHIP FOR SAN ANTONIO PALACE —
PARTIES EMPLOYED DISEMBARKING LUGGAGE

In *En Exil*, Youssoupov summed up the Romanovs' departure from the *Marlborough* in elegant French: *'nous fîmes des
adieux pleins de cordialité et de gratitude au commandant et aux
officiers.'*

Pridham describes the departure briefly in his diary; he
cannot resist alluding to the Dowager's reluctance to leave:
'Started disembarking at 10.00am at which time the Empress
very unwillingly left for San Antonio Palace. Before leaving
she took a group of all the officers of the ship and said goodbye to each in turn.'

Farewells and the exchanging of gifts seem to have gone
ahead, despite the Dowager's continuing confidence that all

the passengers would be re-embarked. Pridham added in his foreword: 'The Empress called me aside and gave me a case containing a magnificent pair of cuff-links – moonstones surrounded by tiny rubies and diamonds. As earrings, brooch and a ring they are now a family heirloom.'

His diary continues: 'The Grand Duchess Xenia and the "boys" went with her [the Dowager], the remainder are being distributed between the various hotels in Sliema. I got them all and their 750 pieces of luggage clear by 3.30 and, marvellous to relate, not a single person or piece of luggage went to the wrong place.' He adds with grim satisfaction: 'Even the Russian servants were kept herded in their correct lots.'

Pridham must have been particularly touched to receive the parting gift of a dagger from one of the Dowager's Cossack guards. The tip of its scabbard was silver-edged; attached to the side of the scabbard was a little eating knife.

As it turned out, Pridham's was not the only Russian dagger to remain on board. One *Marlborough* sailor wrote a jovial letter in February '72 to the BBC: 'Well I can say this, that the time of those Russians were onboard the lads (sailors) were exchanging for one BAR OF SOAP OR A PACKET OF CIGERETTS, we were getting back a sword or a dagger. Well after the opperation, we had to have all arms locked away till we paid off and that was 1 November 1920.' The letter was signed J. Sullivan. 'Please excuse my writing & spelling, thank you.'

Others of the departing passengers seized the opportunity to express their thanks. Pridham was overwhelmed: 'They have insisted on giving a sum of £125 to be distributed among the servants and cooks who have been looking after them. Prince Youssoupov (sen) and Admiral Viazemski endeavoured to make me accept a great deal more than that for them, but I stuck out against it being made too large. I have proposed to the Captain that part of the money be used to provide a memento of the occasion for each and the remainder to be distributed as tips; there are thirty five men concerned altogether.

'One of the greatest successes was the Captain's cook, I was always being congratulated on the dinners. My responsibilities varied from those of Hotel Manager to Naval Adviser to the Empress... Both the Empress and Grand Duchess made charming remarks about the ship when they said goodbye.

'So ends, for the present at any rate, a unique experience for a man-of-war and one we shall none of us forget. The Empress was on board exactly a fortnight, she had never been on board a ship so long in her life and doubtless will never be again.'

But, he still harboured a belief that she would be granted her wish to resume her journey on the *Marlborough*. 'The present arrangement is that they remain at Malta until the *Lord Nelson* arrives from Genoa when they will embark in her and proceed to England. I think myself that we shall shortly receive orders to re-embark most of them and do the trip ourselves.'

The Dowager, as before, made no mention of her hopes in this direction: 'Easter Monday. We were already sitting with our coffee at 9 o'clock as we were due to go ashore at 10 o'clock. I photographed the Captain and all the officers again after which we bade an emotional farewell to our travel companions: the Youssoupovs, the Orloffs, Mengdens and Chatelens, who are all going to stay in town.

'I then said goodbye to everyone and sailed with the Captain behind the docks in order not to see people who I found odd.' By odd people she may simply have meant strangers.

Still unsure of her future plans, the Dowager also presented the Captain with a farewell gift: a cigarette box in the style of Fabergé. The relatively small token may have reflected the lesser attention bestowed upon her by the Captain.

Tom Fothergill, usually so full of stoic good cheer, was clearly put out by the departure of the Romanovs. He seemed to have grown more attached to the passengers than he himself realised.

Though he opens his diary entry and his letter to Punch robustly enough, he ends both on a distinct downbeat. In his diary he wrote: 'Raining a little in morning... cleared up and lovely morning. Started getting the Empress's gear out into drifter. She took a photograph of all of the officers and said goodbye at 10. Guard and band played Russian National Anthem. Started in again at 1.10 with gear going on all afternoon. Finished at 3.30 Everyone out of ship and cabins below taken possession of. Rather sorry now it is all over. Getting ready to coal tomorrow. Mail arrived no letters! Rather a blight with life in general...'

To Punch he wrote: 'So now it is all over and we re-berth the man of war again. It has been an interesting experience – we coal tomorrow a mere 1050 tons and 450 tons of oil and... on Wednesday sailing that day for Constantinople and the Black Sea again such is life! A lot of interesting photographs were taken and I hope to send you some later on.

'It is rather jolly being back in Malta but I'm afraid the stay is rather short, they seem in such a hurry to get us back to the Black Sea and there is nothing very interesting to do there now... not feeling very cheery so will end, the very best of love your loving, loving brother Tom.'

Day 16

Ship's log April 22:
at Malta
09.00 fresh provisions

The Romanov party must have felt relief as they left the Crimea but their arrival in Malta marked the true beginning of the end of their travails.

The British ADC in Malta, Captain Robert Ingham, meticulously recorded his first impressions of the Romanovs in his diary. Perhaps mindful of Russia's recent turmoil, he was particularly struck by the dynamics between masters and servants. He noted how Xenia's sons, the young Princes, rushed to help their beloved Miss Coster off the *Marlborough* with her bags; the actual servants made no effort to help. 'I must have shown some surprise for the eldest of the Princes (Theodor) turned to me and said: "I'm afraid you must think these menservants of ours very lazy and that they have very bad manners, but what is one to expect after two or three years of revolution?"'

The Romanovs were elated by the beauty of the island;

the Dowager was delighted to find herself embroiled once more in social niceties. She continued in her diary: 'There the Admiral met us and then Xenia and I drove in an open motor-car to lovely San Antonio in the loveliest weather and where the air was full of the scent of orange blossoms as we drove into the garden.

'Here we were received by Lord and Lady Methuen, who brought us to our rooms upstairs, which she herself had furnished so beautifully. It was very funny when we went to see where the boys [Xenia's sons] would be accommodated as there were small children's beds since they had thought that they were all young, so we all died of laughter when Lord and Lady Methuen suddenly caught sight of all the big boys!

'It is pure luck that we arrived here some days before the other poor souls; Lord Methuen thought that only peasants and simple people would be coming, so he had arranged everything for them in barracks and hospitals. He almost fell over backwards when I told him that they were all our friends and acquaintances from society who could not possibly be put up in hospitals.'

Pridham underestimated the Dowager's love of these social niceties when he wrote about her arrival in Malta that night. He still expected her to return to the unglamorous life she had evidently so enjoyed on the *Marlborough*. He could hardly restrain a note of smugness: 'I hear the advent of the Empress has turned Malta upside down and resulted in a great number of short tempers, most of the staff have been employed trying to find sheets and pillows suitable for the use of Her Imperial Majesty. Lady Methuen has been at her wits' end and driven most others the same way. It rather amuses me, remembering what they have been so pleased with here, however if they have more suitable arrangements, so much the better.'

The Dowager had visited Malta exactly ten years before, with her sister Alix and King Edward VII. She had enjoyed an endless round of social gatherings, luncheon parties and dinners, missing only one event. According to the *Daily Malta Chronicle* of April 26th, 1909, the event was an opera; the report added tantalisingly that she had missed it because of an unspecified upset: 'her mind was dwelling upon some recent sad occurrence exciting sorrow.'

Now she continued in her diary: 'Everything reminds me so much of our stay here with darling Bertie and Alix... When the same butler presented us with coffee, he said: "It is just ten years ago you arrived today"... The garden has been beautified in the meantime; it is full of flowers and oranges, which are so lovely.'

The Dowager was established in the palace with several servants and her equerry, Serge Dolgorouky, who celebrated his freedom, to the ADC's amusement, by pinning up several 'rather risque' pictures from *La Vie Parisienne*.

Prince Dmitri would retain fond memories of the San Antonio Palace. As he wrote, 'The grounds were full of orange trees and we were able to pick and eat the choicest fruit. The palace was reputed to be haunted not by one, but by several ghosts, including a phantom grey cat. Although our rooms overlooked a terrace which was supposed to be haunted, we saw nothing that worried us.'

'Meals were taken together at a long table in the dining room and our Maltese butler would solemnly announce at the end of each meal "port or marsala" which always amused me.

'On several occasions we took the train to Sliema, just outside Valletta, to visit Russian friends who were staying there. Among them were old Prince and Princess Youssoupov with

Irina and Felix and their daughter.'

He added that a chapel had been thoughtfully converted, by the Governor, into an Orthodox Church and a newly carved altar stone was specially made.

Dmitri's account of their stay in Malta makes no mention of the Princes' bad behaviour, as ruefully noted in Captain Ingham's diary. Aside from the routine antics at mealtimes, the boys snuck out at night over the garden wall and into Valletta. Ingham was obliged in the end to chase them to bed in his pyjamas. 'What a pickle,' he wrote in dismay.

The Dolgoroukys stayed in a hotel in Sliema. The manager seemed to know very little about his guests. He was expecting them to be penniless. As Sofka later wrote: 'Miss King had a favourite story of how the manager of the hotel screened off part of the dining-room so as not to embarrass the poor refugees (the Dolgoroukys), only to find his indigent guests coming down in full, albeit old-fashioned, evening dress and glittering with jewels. Even Miss King was wearing my mother's rope of pearls that she had left during her last visit to the Crimea – but underneath her inevitable high-necked blouses...'

Sofka was very taken with Malta: 'I enjoyed Malta. There were morning walks with Miss King watching the women come running out of the houses with jugs as the goat-herd's bell resounded. Then the pause as jugs were filled straight from the udder and coins passed from hand to hand, before the flock was driven on with incomprehensible cries.

'In the afternoon we would accompany Granny in an open fiacre to visit the caves of St Paul, the chapel of bones or out to some point down the dusty roads of the island.'

The Youssoupovs, like the Dolgoroukys, were in a hotel; Felix Youssoupov was in raptures, describing, 'vast gardens on terraces'. He mentions: 'It was only now that we became fully conscious that our lives were no longer under threat. Joie de vivre returned with this feeling of security.

'That night my brother-in-law Theodor and I did a tour of all the nightclubs in the town. A great fuss was made of the passengers from the *Marlborough*. A group of English and American sailors, singing at the tops of their voices, took us from bar to bar each time offering us a drink. After several hours of that regime, we judged it wise to return before finding ourselves out of our heads.'

The sailors from the *Marlborough*, meanwhile, went ashore for more demure pursuits. Marine George Gravestock, who had picked a rose at Koreiz for his fiancée, now had a handsome photograph taken of himself at Valletta. Several months later, he sent it to her: 'To my Dearest Ethel, with fondest love from George August 5 1919.' Pridham had his own urgent matters to attend to: '...Went ashore in the evening to replenish my wardrobe which has been rather severely taxed recently.'

The following day, on April 23rd, Pridham's hopes of the Romanovs returning to the *Marlborough* were dashed. One of the officers, Lieutenant Moore, had gone to San Antonio to give the Dowager some photographs of the ship. In his diary, Pridham described how Moore returned with the disappointing news. The Romanovs, he was told, were to continue to England, as originally proposed, on the *Lord Nelson*. The Dowager was of course upset by the King's refusal to change the plan. She would have seen it, not least, as a slight. 'She has had a reply from the King saying that he much regretted that the *Marlborough* is urgently required elsewhere,' wrote Pridham. 'So much for that then, but I am sorry we could not finish off the job properly. Left for Constantinople in the evening. Some of the young Princes came on board to say goodbye.'

The decision to transfer the Dowager to the *Lord Nelson* was, in the end political. The *Lord Nelson* was due to return to England; diverting the *Marlborough* to England would have been expensive and controversial. Pridham gave a slightly sour explanation: 'Evidently it was thought to be important to avoid giving further opportunity for criticism in incurring unnecessary expenditure.'

❧

It was during the Romanovs' week in Malta that the Dowager received a curious visit from a British agent called Major William Peer Groves. Distinguished, according to a subsequent BBC investigation, by 'heavy black eyebrows', he gave her some sort of keepsake, apparently proving to her that her son, the Tsar, and his family were still alive.

The *Marlborough* crew was obviously not directly involved in any of these machinations but curiously, amongst Fothergill's papers, there is a scruffy piece of notepaper with a memo written in pencil from Peer Groves.

MALTA
DATED 4.3.19
MAJOR PEER GROVES (HQ RAF MALTA)
TO CAPT. HMS TEMERAIRE

I AM IN SS 'PETER THE GREAT' WITH TWO RUSSIAN OFFICERS ON A SPECIAL MISSION. I HAVE CONFIDENTIAL PAPERS AND REPORTS FOR C IN C AND INTELLIGENCE GHQ. I AM TO REPORT TO COB IN ORDER TO ARRANGE FOR IMMEDIATE TRANSPORT TO MALTA.

CAN YOU SEND A BOAT PLEASE?

I AM NOT AU FAIT WITH THE PORT REGULATIONS AS
TO MILITARY PASSENGERS DISEMBARKING FOR RE-
EMBARKATION BUT MY BUSINESS IS VERY URGENT AND
IMPORTANT AND DELAY IS TO BE AVOIDED IF POSSIBLE.

W. PEER GROVES   MAJOR RAF'

Years later, conspiracists, who argued for the secret survival of the Tsar and his family, tried to prove that the Dowager was more cheerful on the second leg of her journey to
England, on the *Lord Nelson*. And three days after Peer Groves'
meeting with the Dowager in Malta, she certainly had an intriguing conversation with Captain Ingham. This conversation, over dinner, was distinctly different from the one she had
had with Pridham on the *Marlborough*. As Ingham recorded:
'I was rather surprised when Her Majesty began to talk about
her son – the Tsar – and told me that she was careful not to let
others know but that she knew where he was.

'HIM was fully convinced that he had escaped and was in
hiding at a certain place. I think the family had encouraged
her to believe the Tsar was still alive and they looked at me
rather pointedly when Her Majesty was telling me about him,
so I was careful to let her think we were all convinced she was
right.'

Before leaving Malta, the Dowager visited several courtiers who had been installed in altogether lowlier accommodation; some of them were in barracks, with two or three to a
room, reduced to living like 'peasants and simple people'. As
one recalled reverentially: 'On the eve of Her departure for
England, the Empress announced Her wish to visit all the barracks and camps in which we were accommodated in the envi-
rons of the city. Our happiness at seeing Her was clouded by
inexpressible sorrow at parting from Her. The next day, with

heavy hearts, we watched as the dreadnought sailed away into the distance, bearing our Mother Empress.'

The *Marlborough*'s Captain Johnson was among the party to meet the Dowager at the quay. He accompanied her on the launch to the *Lord Nelson*. The likelihood was that he felt more relief than regret at being shot of a peculiarly onerous responsibility.

Half a century after the fateful *Marlborough* journey, in the 1970s, a BBC programme investigated the possibility that some of the Tsar's immediate family might have survived the massacre at Ekaterinburg. At this point, members of the former crew of the *Marlborough* and the *Lord Nelson* weighed in with confusing testimony. At least two seemed to have been convinced that the Tsar's daughter, Grand Duchess Anastasia, was among the party of Romanovs to escape from the Crimea.

An NT Cooper from the *Marlborough* wrote to the *Telegraph*: 'I know that the Tsar, with or without beard, was not in the party my ship brought away from Russia and there was no other ship involved in the operation (which was by command of HM the King).'

But a marine from the *Lord Nelson*, J Mitchell, of Dinton, Wilts, wrote convinced that Anastasia had been among the Dulbers picked up from Constantinople. Claimed Mitchell: 'In the party was a girl who was much younger than her fellow-refugees. This girl was pointed out to me by servants as Anastasia, the Czar's youngest daughter.' He enclosed a picture of a young woman seated on a chair: in fact, Marina, sitting next to her mother, the Grand Duchess

Militsa, while her father stands behind.

Similarly, a sailor from the *Marlborough*, JH Barber of Bournemouth, wrote saying: 'Embarking aboard the *Marlborough* with the Empress and Grand Duke was very many other people who it was understood to be members of the Russian Royalty, one of which, it was said, many months after, was the young princess of the Tsar who escaped to USA and eventually died there.' Actually, the most famous Anastasia claimant, Anna Anderson, died in America much later, in 1984.

There should not have been any confusion, as all the sailors were given a printed list of the people in the party. 'Each member of the ship's company was given one,' claimed HM Bennett, of Beacon Lough East, Gateshead.

Pridham himself finally wrote to the BBC: 'You probably know that there has been a long drawn out endeavour by interested [for gain] parties to bring forward a woman as being the Grand Duchess Anastasia, the youngest of the Emperor Nicholas II's daughters. There is however no doubt that the real Anastasia was murdered and her body burnt at the same time and in the same place as were the others of the Imperial Family imprisoned at Ekaterinburg... There have been many false stories conjured up by those endeavouring to make money out of that page of Russian history.'

Nonetheless, conspiracists remained intrigued by the Dowager's high spirits on the *Lord Nelson*. Some of the crew particularly noted the difference between her mood and that of the Dulbers, who had been on board just a week before. According to Michael B Laing, then a junior officer, now living in Royston, the Empress was 'a gay old spark... in fact didn't seem to care a crack... I think she had quite a roving eye for good-looking young doctors and men of that sort, though she was no chicken... she wore a pair of abominable yellow boots... she was much more "bobish" and excitable, more alive, than Queen Alexandra, who was dignified and quiet.

'On one occasion she had dinner with the Captain and said that the officers will dance. The Captain was slightly horrified and said "Well really Madam, the chaps are on watch," and all that, and she said she couldn't help that, and out came the Marine band, and I got up, and we gathered on the quarter deck and started to dance, and that's all there was to it.' She apparently enjoyed the proceedings from a perch on the after capstan.

It was a Mr Douglas who described the contrast in mood between the two Romanov parties: 'Her party was so convivial where the other party was full of sorrow... She was pretty talkative to all and sundry... and seemed to take part in all the fun.'

Nor could the Dowager's spirits on the *Lord Nelson* be dampened by weather so rough that it defeated her trusty Cossacks. The *Morning Post* made the most of the men's humiliating plight. Under the headline: 'Helpless Royal Bodyguard... Seasick Cossacks', the *Post* reported: 'the passage was distinctly rough, particularly so during the crossing of the Bay of Biscay. Yet it made no impression on the venerable passenger of 71 years. She sat tranquilly throughout the stormiest periods, enjoying her cigarette and a glass of wine.

'But the faithful bodyguard of four' – actually two – 'stalwart Cossacks had no sea-legs. Men of commanding physique, they were helpless during the whole voyage and cut pathetic figures. Their relief on reaching Portsmouth was unbounded.'

Prince Dmitri also recalled his grandmother's fortitude as she confronted the vagaries of the ocean: 'The day was quite sunny but the sea was rough. As she was sitting in the sunshine in her chair a large wave suddenly crashed across the deck drenching her from head to foot. She took it very well and laughed so much that she was unable to get up from her chair for quite a while. We also laughed a lot at the sight of her sitting there in a bedraggled hat and fur coat.'

Little Sofka Dolgorouky was *bouleversé* in a different way. A suspicious-sounding sailor called Geoffrey took a shine to her and seems to have visited her ashore, kissing her behind bushes. 'He must have been 17 at the time and I was 11 so there could really have been no mutual plane of contact... for the next couple of years he would come and see me whenever on leave, wrote constantly and his kisses were not entirely platonic...

'After that he disappeared quite suddenly... I had thoroughly enjoyed it without having what we termed "a crush" (he had too many teeth) so that I was in no way bruised, but rather astonished at his vanishing.' Ten years later she read that her sailor had been killed in Switzerland flying his Moth.

❧

On May 22nd, a naval signal was sent from Constantinople to the *Marlborough*.

From Admiralty. London.
For Captain Johnson HMS Marlborough
Let me once more express to you the most
heartfelt and grateful thanks for all your
kindness shown me by you and your Officers
aboard your beautiful Marlborough which
so helped us all. My only regret is you

COULD NOT BRING US ALL HERE. MANY KIND
REGARDS TO YOU ALL,
  MARIE FEODOROVNA

FROM MARLBOROUGH
TO: ADMIRALTY FOR DOWAGER, EMPRESS OF RUSSIA
MARLBOROUGH THANKS YOU GRATEFULLY FOR KIND
MESSAGE. ALL HANDS WERE FORTUNATE TO HAVE BEEN
OF SERVICE TO YOU AND WE TRUST YOU MAY ENJOY
REST AFTER YOUR SEVERE TRIALS.

Captain Johnson retained a handwritten, undated letter
from Buckingham Palace :

Dear Captain Johnson,
I am commanded by the King to thank you and your
officers in His Majesty's name for the attention paid to the
Empress Maria and for the arrangements made for her
comfort and convenience. The Empress has expressed to
the King in very warm terms her gratitude for all that was
done for her on board the *Marlborough*.
Yours sincerely,
Charles L Cust.

But the Romanovs' *Marlborough* rescue did not quite
end with these formalities. Before the close of 1919, several of the ship's officers had shown they were not about to
forego the romantic drama in which they had found themselves. At least two conducted altogether warmer exchanges
with their former passengers.

On October 17th, 1919, Lieutenant Alan Sheffield wrote
a cheerful and notably relaxed letter to Grand Duchess
Xenia, sending photographs and apologising for the six

months' delay in their arrival. 'The fact of my not having sent them before must have caused you to form a very bad opinion, for which I'm very sorry indeed; but really it has been impossible... The story of misadventure is a long one, which in the telling may be irksome but before you condemn me I ask you to listen. You already know that the negatives had to be sent to England for printing. This was done shortly after you left the ship, which then went to Constantinople and thence to Kaffa Bay (Gulf of Theodosia)...

'From what I have seen of Russia I think it is a beautiful country (with the exception of Marinapol) and I was very sorry to leave it. I am hoping that perhaps the *Marlborough* may go back, but I am afraid it is unlikely – worst luck!' At the bottom of the letter Sheffield writes '*Dasvidanya*' (goodbye) in Cyrillic lettering.

When Francis Pridham's third daughter was born, a few months later, he wrote to the Dowager's equerry, Prince Serge Dolgorouky, asking for permission to name the new arrival after her: 'Marie'. While he did not need permission, he would have relished the nod to etiquette. More importantly, it was a way of re-establishing contact. To this end he also asked the Dowager if she would be little Joan Marie's godmother. A telegram came back saying that the Empress graciously agreed to be godmother. The christening took place on board the *Marlborough* on December 21st, 1919.

The historic grandeur of their mission perhaps compensated lowlier members of the crew for any immediate disappointments. As J Sullivan wrote from Upper Clapton, London E5, in 1972: 'Only there was a rumure [sic] that we would get a medal, things were so secret that we never got it.'

The *Marlborough*'s Russian experience was by no means

over. Later in 1919, the ship rescued General Denikin, whose Cossack soldiers performed war dances on decks. A sailor on the HMS *Montrose* recalled the dances: 'July or August 1919 as we had Quarter Deck awning up, being rather warm at the time the general's staff gave us an exhibition of a Cossack war dance, finishing off with revolvers shooting up through awning. I know that we scarpered forward... on Kertch we actually saw a man hung up on a lamp-post with cigarette ends in his mouth, whether he was Bolshie or Loyalist I never knew! I Remain Yours sincerely Mr EG Golding, of Barking, Essex.'

The Dowager's life in exile began with suitable poignancy. When the party was finally greeted by King George and Queen Mary at Victoria Station, one of the Romanov servants mistook the King for the Tsar. As the cousins exchanged greetings, the servant threw herself at the King's knee. According to a friend of Vassily's, the family never forgot it: 'it was embarrassing for the Empress and Xenia. Vassily found it excruciating.'

Though the Dowager and her sister Alix had earlier enjoyed an emotional reunion at Portsmouth, they soon began getting on each other's nerves. They tried to make a go of things, living together at Marlborough House and entertaining Xenia and her sons for lunch every Sunday. Xenia and her sons were by then living in a four-storey terraced house in Chelsea. But the Queen was tardy and deaf, while the Dowager was beset by arthritis, lumbago and an uncertain income.

The Dowager was upset by what she perceived as the British indifference to the plight of the Russian refugees; and no less put out by her fellow exiles themselves, who, she felt, had let standards of protocol slip.

Within just a few months of her arrival, the disgruntled Dowager had decided that she wanted to return to her homeland of Denmark. By August 1919 she was on her way. The news would have been greeted with some relief; she had already become persona non grata within certain political circles. She herself was ecsatic: 'Better number one at Hvidore [a Royal residence in Denmark] than number two at Sandringham' she crowed.

Unfortunately, her problems did not end in Denmark, where she found her nephew King Christian persistently disagreeable. At one point he told her to switch off some of her lights at the Amalienborg Palace: she was using up too much electricity. Affronted, she immediately ordered the servants to switch all her lights on. In 1920 she gave up the struggle and finally settled at Hvidore, where her number one status may have provided compensation for the humbler surroundings.

She had little financial security; she had hung onto her jewels but these she refused to sell, telling the family peremptorily that they would inherit everything when she had gone. Hopes raised by the early arrival, from the Anitchkov Palace in St Petersburg, of two heavy trunks, were soon dashed. As one biographer put it: 'the case was full to the top with rusty fire-irons, common pokers, shovels and tongs'; the second case contained 'harness and saddlery, old mouldy and perished, broken straps, missing buckles, burst and torn saddles'.

The Dowager and Alix met for the last time when she came to England in 1923 for the marriage of the King's second son Albert, Duke of York, to Elizabeth Bowes-Lyon at Westminster Abbey. The Dowager became ill during her visit and was obliged to remain in England for several months, doubtless to the irritation of both sisters.

The issue of who was to be the Russian heir rose periodically. The Dowager, still refusing to believe that the Tsar was dead, would not countenance any discussion: 'Up to now there has been no reliable information about the fate of my beloved sons and grandchildren. I think, therefore, that it is premature to elect a new emperor. The last glimpse of hope may still be allowed me.' In 1921 she had been offered the locum tenens of the Russian throne by the All Russian Monarchical Assembly. She had simply retorted: 'Nobody saw Nicky killed.'

Various courtiers left accounts of conversations, in which the Dowager made shadowy references to the Tsar. Countess Mengden wrote: 'She told me once: "When I look back on my life and what I have lived through I cannot but believe in ghosts."'; Captain Daneilbach, a member of the Royal entourage said: 'we often heard her say: "In Russia even the most improbable can happen".'

But, in 1924, her controversial cousin, Grand Duke Kyril, had the temerity to declare himself, first, Guardian of the Throne, then, a month later, Emperor of all the Russias. Kyril was already regarded with opprobrium by most of the Romanovs after he had flown a red flag from the roof of his palace while the Tsar was still in power.

The Dowager was incandescent. In the spirit – at last – of my enemy's enemy is my friend, she made a passionate appeal to Nikolasha, casting aside all her old grievances. She wrote: 'I was most terribly pained when I read Grand Duke Kyril Vladmirovich's manifesto proclaiming himself EMPEROR OF ALL THE RUSSIAS.

'To date there has been no precise information concerning the fate of My beloved Sons or My Grandson and for this reason, I consider the proclamation of a new EMPEROR to be premature. There is still no one who could ever extinguish in me the last ray of hope.

'I fear that this manifesto will create division. This will not improve the situation but, quite the opposite, will worsen it, while Russia is tormented enough without such a thing.

'If it has pleased THE LORD GOD, as he acts in HIS mysterious ways, to summon My beloved sons and grandson to HIMSELF then, without wishing to look ahead and with firm hope in the mercy of GOD, I believe that HIS MAJESTY THE EMPEROR will be elected in accordance with Our Basic Laws by the Orthodox Church in concert with the Russian People... I am sure that, as the senior member of the HOUSE OF THE ROMANOVS, You are of the same opinion as Myself. Maria'

She died in 1928, in the presence of her daughters, Xenia and Olga, and one of Xenia's sons. According to Xenia's husband, Sandro, she was clutching her Danish Bible. This was the same Bible confiscated by revolutionary sailors in the Crimea and apparently returned to her in Copenhagen shortly before her death. Her grandson, Prince Dmitri, added that it had been sent by a Danish diplomat who had found it in a book shop in Moscow.

The *Times* obituary paid tribute to the Dowager, giving the lie to the memory of at least one of her grandchildren. One of her daughter Olga's sons would recall bitterly: 'everything belonged to my grandmother and only existed for her. Everybody else including me was nothing.'

But the *Times* maintained: 'During her long life, she experienced the sharpest changes of fortune... She moved in the centre of tragedy. Yet in her nature there was nothing tragic. She preserved throughout a simplicity and sweetness of disposition, a resilience and a quiet incredulity that protected her against the worst shocks.'

Immediately after her death, her two loyal Cossacks, Timofei Yachik and Kyril Poliakoff, stood guard as she lay in state in the Garden Room of the palace in Copenhagen.

Timofei had accompanied his mistress first to London then to Copenhagen. He had parted from her only briefly when he returned to Russia on a secret mission to help rescue her daughter Olga, and her husband and two sons. It was during this visit that he had seen his wife and daughters for the last time. When he returned to Copenhagen, he decided to settle in Denmark permanently. While the decision may have been prompted by his loyalty to the Dowager, he would have had little choice: in Soviet Russia he would obviously have been a marked man. His wife died in 1922. He married again three years later.

After the Dowager's death, Timofei received a sizeable £8 a month from the British Court until 1938. On the strength of this legacy, he opened a small grocery ship with his wife. He died in 1946.

In a recent exhibition in Copenhagen, 'Russian Full Dress Uniforms from Empress Maria Feodorovna's Time', the Cossacks' section featured Timofei's leather brown gun holster, some medals, old rouble notes never changed and purple stone cuff-links which had belonged to the Tsar.

And there was a certificate signed by the equerry, Serge Dolgorouky, given to Timofei upon the death of the Dowager. Entitled 'Cossack Bodyguard Certificate', the document read: 'This certificate given as proof that Timofei served as Cossack from 3 Dec 1915 until her death on 30 Sept/13 Oct 1928.' His enlarged cutlery was also on display.

Prince Viazemski, the former Admiral of the Russian

Navy, whose impotence the Dowager had bewailed on the *Marlborough*, also accompanied his mistress to Copenhagen where he acted as a sort of Chancellor to her Court. He died in Copenhagen, aged 68, of heart trouble.

In September 2006 the Dowager's body, originally buried at Roskilde, was taken in a Danish warship to Peterhof in Russia. After lying in state at St Isaac's Cathedral, she was finally interred in the vault of the Peter and Paul Fortress in St Petersburg with the remains of the Tsar, Tsarina and five children.

Throughout her life in exile, Grand Duchess Xenia struggled to maintain aspects of her former life. She began painting again, selling some of her work for charity. She clung to her Russian servants, especially the laundrywoman Anna Belousoff. The optimistic Belousoff, who had once boasted ten of her own laundry girls and a cook, kept a trunk permanently packed, ready for an imminent return to Russia. As Prince Dmitri recalled: 'She used to say "we're going back", this went on until she died aged over 90.'

But Xenia's nostalgia for the past had to be fitted around more pressing matters, not least her precarious finances. In 1921 the trusty tutor, Mr Stewart, helped her open a bank account at Coutts. But this got off to a bad start: with £1,000 credit she promply spent £98 in Harrods, the equivalent today of £2,000. That same year an unfortunate encounter with an American conman cost her £10,000. He had promised her millions if she would invest in a photographic printing process. He was arrested after defrauding a woman of her watch, sent to prison for three months and deported back to America.

At this point, King George V decided to step in, agreeing to grant his cousin £2,400 a year. In 1925 he took the additional step of installing her in a house at Frogmore. Her letter of thanks is effusive to the point of being flirtatious: 'Really Georgie, it is too good and kind of you. I longed to write at once and have written and torn up many sheets of paper but felt shy! And didn't quite know what was going on.' Had she ever known the details of Georgie's failure to rescue her brother, the Tsar, she might not have felt so well disposed towards him.

While her immediate practical needs were met, Xenia faced a further, unexpected series of blows. After Lenin's death in 1924, the Bolsheviks began selling off confiscated goods. Treasures formerly belonging to the Imperial Family now appeared in England. At one point, an acquaintance of Xenia's showed her a rose jade box embossed with an Imperial crown. 'I would be curious to know whose initials those are,' he said. When Xenia replied: 'They're mine,' the man, a collector, put the box back in his window without further comment.

On another occasion, Queen Mary produced a pink onyx Fabergé box designed to hold cards for patience. She asked Xenia what she thought of it. Xenia immediately recognised it and said: 'That used to be on my writing desk.' Whereupon Queen Mary replaced the box in a cabinet. As it turns out, Queen Mary would not have been in the least put out to be told that the card box belonged to somebody else. Her passion for acquiring other people's possessions was so well known that treasures were carefully hidden before her visits.

In 1928, Xenia's misery over her mother's death would have been compounded with the stepping-up of a campaign supporting a woman claiming to be her niece, the Tsar's youngest daughter Anastasia. The subsequent lawsuit, which muddied the already murky waters of Xenia's money worries, would drag on for a harrowing 50 years. The issue of inheritance could not be settled until it was accepted that the Tsar, Tsarina and all five children were dead. In the 1930s, Xenia was visited by her cousin, Princess Xenia Leeds, who believed in the claimant; the Princess had put 'Anastasia' up for several months on her Long Island estate. 'Anastasia', she claimed, had recognised her cousin Prince Dmitri's voice as he shouted on the tennis court.

Over the next few years, tragedy jostled with small cares as Xenia struggled to claim payments for basins, cooking apparatus and a hot water service from the British Government. The bills would first go to the Treasury, from where they would be smartly dispatched to the Palace. 'As the Grand Duchess is very poor,' the Keeper of the Privy Purse would explain starkly, 'the King has been in the habit of paying for alterations and improvements.'

For years King George V had attempted to 'contain' Xenia to keep her expenses down. But in 1934 an outbreak of scarlet fever at Frogmore eventually resulted in the King's successor, King Edward VIII, suggesting that Xenia move to Wilderness House, at Hampton Court: doctors had been alarmed to find more than 20 house guests at Frogmore.

An Orthodox chapel was duly constructed in the drawing room of Wilderness House and Xenia was satisfactorily resettled, sharing none of Capability Brown's disparaging views of the 'small uncomfortable rooms, offensive kitchen and bad offices'.

In 1938, the Russian flavour of Xenia's household was enhanced with the addition of a Russian mystic. The new arrival was called Mother Martha. 'She is a nun... Bertie and Elizabeth know her,' Xenia wrote briefly to Queen Mary. Mother Martha was to become a 'controversial figure in the family', as Xenia's grandson, Alexander, put it. The young

Grand Duchess Xenia, second from left, with Princess Irina and her sons. Dmitri is second from the right, and Vassily is on the left

English Princesses, Elizabeth and Margaret, had been very taken with their Russian relation, merrily singing the 'Volga Boat Song' whenever they passed Xenia's house. Now they were further struck by Mother Martha, particularly noting her large feet. Both sisters thought she was a man.

James Pope-Hennessey, who visited Xenia in the late 1950s, echoed the sisters' thoughts; he gave an elaborate description of Mother Martha's appearance. She wore 'on her head a coif of unstarched and indeed crumpled linen of the tea-cloth variety, tied at the back of the head with two tapes. She has the face of a powerful elderly man'. After barely 20 minutes, Pope-Hennessey and Xenia were interrupted by Mother Martha, who tried to bring their interview to a close. Pope-Hennessey subsequently likened the Grand Duchess to an 'exceedingly nervous wild bird... trapped'. It was a mark either of Xenia's generosity of spirit or her naiveté that she felt sorry for the looming nun, who, she claimed, was 'reduced to this kind of existence, her health ruined, nerves all shattered and I sit and look on, sick at heart and worried beyond words and unwell myself'.

At the centre of the two women's worries were domestic upsets, not least a row between a nanny, Narnya, a successor to Miss Coster, and a recalcitrant cook who, as Xenia complained to her sister, 'uses up any amount of pans and retires to her room leaving everything in a mess... no *humilité chrétienne.*'

Visits from the gallant Pridham must have provided a welcome diversion. His devotion meant that he fully supported Mother Martha, indeed, compared her to 'our own Florence Nightingale'. He acknowledged that there was some difficulty with her identity: 'Although I know that she comes from a Russian family of high degree, I do not know and may not discover this lady's true name.'

Pridham and Xenia clearly both enjoyed their decorous conversations over tea, and he left only the most respectful personal impressions. Prince David Chavchavadze, who saw her for the last time in 1956, had no such scruples: 'Xenia chain-smoked the whole time, flicking cigarette butts into what she called a "small spitoon" about four feet away. She never missed once.'

Aged over 80, Xenia summoned the ADC Captain Ingham to Wilderness House on his visit to England from Malta at the end of 1958. She told him she and her mother had lost their hearts to his 'lovely island and people' and that they had even asked the King if they could live in Malta. She added that the Queen and Prince Philip had continued the tradition of kindness from the British Royal Family and had recently brought Prince Charles and Princess Anne to have tea with her.

Apparently, the Royal party was served tea on a tray by Xenia's grandson Alexander. As Ingham enthused: 'He had been downstairs to the kitchen to make the tea and cut the bread and butter himself!'

Xenia died at Hampton Court on April 20th, 1960, surrounded by adoring grandsons. According to one biography: 'Mother Martha appeared carrying a box marked "black mourning veils" kept in readiness for such eventualities.' After the funeral she disappeared.

Xenia left £117,272.16 shillings and tuppence. She was buried at Roquebrune near Nice, next to her husband Sandro. In the end she was not granted her wish to be buried at Ai-Todor; but Roquebrune was chosen, according to her son Dmitri, because of its resemblance to the Crimea.

In his unpublished memoir, completed years later, Prince Dmitri began the description of his life in exile with vivid memories of his first few days in England: 'We were driven straight to Buckingham Palace, where we were met on arrival by the Prince of Wales, the future King Edward VIII, who was standing at the entrance door to the palace. He escorted us to our rooms, making polite conversation as we went, and he surprised me by asking which way we had crossed the Channel, via Calais or Boulogne...

'That first night in London did not seem so strange. The atmosphere of one palace is much like another and being in one in London, with our English relatives, helped obscure the reality of the situation, making St Petersburg seem less far away than before.'

Dmitri as yet knew nothing of the King's failure to rescue his uncle. So when – as he made a habit of doing at the time – the King hid his shame by uttering ever louder condemnations of Lloyd George, Dmitri never doubted his sincerity. As he wrote: 'I twice heard King George refer to Lloyd George as "that murderer" in the presence of my mother. Years later I asked the Duke of Windsor "Who was it that your father called 'that murderer'?" and he had no trouble remembering.'

In other respects, however, Dmitri formed a bad impression of the King, who, he felt, bullied his children. He recalled the King becoming impatient with Prince Albert (later George VI) because of his stammer and teasing Prince Henry for his lack of facial hair: 'Look at him he can't even grow a moustache.' He never forgave his daughter, Princess Mary, for having feet bigger than his: 'Look at her – she can't wear my shoes.'

The young Dmitri cast an equally acute but more sympathetic eye upon Queen Mary, who had damaged her knee when young: 'she had learnt to walk with a special sideways gait which helped disguise her disability.'

As Dmitri contemplated his future, Mr Stewart once again came to the rescue. He showed him round Queen's College, Oxford. The college later offered Dmitri a place, and by the autumn of 1919, he was installed in a crammer on Hayling Island.

Dmitri subsequently enjoyed a rich professional life; his first ventures were in New York, where he worked as a stockbroker and sold ties. At one point, he smuggled scotch and gin, in the course of which he claimed to have met Al Capone. His distinctive name presented him with quandaries. As a young man, he disliked 'Romanov' because it had too many associations. But his preferred choice of 'Prince Dmitri' led to further difficulties, not least mishearing. His new acquaintances would frequently reply: 'Pleased to meet you too.'

After moving back to Europe, he worked for Coco Chanel and, in November 1931, married a Chanel model who was, more importantly, a White Russian aristocrat: Countess Marina Golenitscheff-Koutouzov.

During the war he joined the Navy. It is hard to know to what extent he retained the boyhood fascination with battleships which had so gratified the *Marlborough* crew. But he rose swiftly to Lieutenant Commander and helped with the evacuation of Dunkirk; he made two journeys, each time rescuing 700 to 800 men.

He served as Naval Attaché to the Royal Hellenic and Royal Yugoslav Navies, which were stationed in British waters, and accompanied the Allied Naval Attachés on two trips to Paris immediately after the Liberation. King George VI graciously wrote a letter in May 1940, carefully conserved by Dmitri, in which he professed himself 'glad you're in the RN'. Years later, in his memoir, Pridham paid tribute to Dmitri's successful Naval career: He 'served with distinction throughout the war, being gifted with a natural ability for leadership.'

After the war, Dmitri's formerly chequered career resumed as he became, first, Secretary of the Travellers Club in Paris and then European sales representative of Seagram's Whisky. While in Paris, he became close to the Duke and Duchess of Windsor and when, in 1954, he married his second wife Sheila Chisholm, he proudly reported Wallis's comment: 'think what you like, but I fixed this marriage.' The couple celebrated with a religious ceremony at the tiny chapel of Wilderness House, in the presence of Xenia and the ubiquitous Mother Martha.

Dmitri wrote enthusiastically about his *Marlborough* journey. During the 1950s, he helped Pridham with his memoir, revealing, not least, the secret behind his astonishingly detailed knowledge of battleships. As Pridham wrote: 'He has since told me he never moved without taking a copy of *Jane's Fighting Ships* with him, so that I suspect that at the time he slept with it under his pillow.'

Dmitri always refused a British passport. According to his granddaughter, there were two reasons for this. First, he expected, on some level, to return to and settle in Russia; secondly, he never quite shook off his doubts about the British, particularly their failure to rescue his uncle. When he finally had the opportunity to visit Russia in his old age, he refused: 'I would not want to see it as it is now.'

In his last years, he overcame his reservations about his surname sufficiently to become President of the Romanov Dynasty Family Association. He died, aged 79, in July 1980, in the King Edward VII Hospital in London.

Prince Dmitri's granddaughter, Penny Galitzine, now lives near Hailsham, in Sussex. She came to London from Canada as a student, aged 20, and met her grandfather on a daily basis. She is now fond keeper of his extensive collection of papers, including his sister Princess Irina's paintings of mushrooms.

In 1998, she attended the burial of the Romanov family remains in St Petersburg; she says she found herself particularly moved as the mourners followed the route the Imperial Family had taken on their last journey to the station.

Dmitri's youngest brother, Prince Vassily, was educated in Europe, then travelled to New York with his father 'two weeks before the crash', as he put it. While he never followed his brother into the Navy, he betrayed their shared maritime passion with jobs as a cabin boy and shipyard worker.

His subsequent professional life echoed his brother's in terms of diversity. After a stint also as a stockbroker, he settled in California, where he made wine near San Jose and bred chickens in Sonoma. He once said: 'In my colourful career, I think I enjoyed the chicken farm the best.' In 1931, he met and married a Hollywood film actress, Natasha Galitzine, in New York. Natasha, in common with most of her sisters-in-law, came from a distinguished White Russian family.

Vassily retained the good humour so much in evidence on the *Marlborough*. He was generally unsentimental. Though he carefully kept an amber frog given him by his great aunt Alix, he had no compunction about selling the Cross of St George Fabergé egg that the Dowager had stowed on the *Marlborough*. He inherited the egg upon the death of his mother in 1960. After the Dowager's death, it had passed on to Xenia, who lent it to organisers of a Fabergé exhibition in a private house in Belgravia in 1936. Vassily sold it for £16,000 to Fabergé Inc. It was then bought by the magazine magnate, Malcolm Forbes.

In 1984 he told an interviewer: 'I just thank God we're here. We still have a pretty free country. God bless America.' Regarding the Gorbachev reforms, he was quoted as saying simply: 'It's a very exciting time we live in.' Within 18 months of Vassily's death, Gorbachev had presided over the final dismantling of the Soviet Union.

Vassily's resilient spirit was at least partly attributable to his religious faith. His friend Albert Bartridge now says: 'Vassily never lost his faith but he was not a regular church-goer. He was a private, quiet person and other worshippers wouldn't let him alone.' Vassily kept an icon from the Dowager in his bedroom. He died of natural causes aged 81, in bed in June 1989 – in the Woodside home where he had lived for 25 years.

The Princes' Miss Coster enjoyed the privilege of

being the only nanny mentioned in Pridham's account of the *Marlborough* journey. The loyalty that had so impressed Pridham on that first night on board continued as a feature of Miss Coster's life back in England. She named her house in Eastbourne after Xenia's house in the Crimea, Ai-Todor. According to Prince Dmitri, the name was spelt incorrectly but, as he added with some pride: 'we never told her.' She died in the late 1930s.

Prince Felix Youssoupov's early years in exile were spent with his wife Irina in Knightsbridge, in the flat that he had bought during his student days at Oxford. Among the acquaintances he saw soon after his arrival in England was Duff Cooper. On September 11th, 1919, Cooper wrote a curmudgeonly note in his diary: 'I hadn't seen him for years. He seemed in no way altered by having murdered Rasputin but rather sillier.'

Youssoupov was extremely conscientious towards his fellow White Russians; food and clothes parcels were packed up and sent back to Russia for the White Army. He gave money directly to exiles and at one point bought a house for them. According to one friend, his generosity was such that he would leave himself with no money even to buy light bulbs. The couple kept an open house, with a stream of Russian visitors who would apparently speak Italian in order to discuss art and English in order to discuss sport. Perhaps it was as well that the pet parrot, Mary, didn't try to speak at all.

His generosity may have been linked to his firm belief, during his first year of exile, that the Russian monarchy was about to be restored. As Duff Cooper wrote of a dinner party on July 21st, 1921: 'Felix came with his pockets full of diamonds and pearls which he wants to sell. He is confident that he will be back in Russia under a Tsar within a year.'

In his memoirs, Youssoupov recorded that, on one occasion, he was singing and playing guitar in a room at the Ritz Hotel, when there was an urgent knock at the door: 'I thought it was an irritated neighbour, but it was Grand Duke Dmitri, who I had not seen since "l'affaire Rasputine". He had recognised my voice through the wall.' Youssoupov and Grand Duke Dmitri (his cousin by marriage) had been the central conspirators in the murder of Rasputin. The pair resumed their friendship until 1954, when Youssoupov published a lurid memoir. Grand Duke Dmitri thought Youssoupov had broken the agreement they had made not to discuss the murder plot publicly. He never spoke to Youssoupov again.

Through the 1920s, Youssoupov found himself extremely short of money and agreed to an unusual deal regarding his two Rembrandt portraits. He was to lend the paintings to a dealer in return for $400,000. Until a certain date, he could buy them back at the same price, but if, by then, he had not bought them back, they became the property of the dealer. The deal came unstuck and the Youssoupovs were obliged to take their jewels to New York in a bid to fight the case. But they lost, and the paintings ended up in the National Gallery of Art in Washington.

The loss of the two Rembrandts followed the seizure of a whole collection of paintings, 1,147 in all, by the Bolsheviks from the Youssoupovs' palace in St Petersburg. Within five years of the Revolution, the Bolsheviks had unearthed most of the family's hidden treasure, not least a collection of 128 violins, including a Stradivarius, concealed in a column. On his deathbed, Youssoupov's valet revealed further details of a strong room, the entrance to which was concealed behind a bookcase. Here, the Bolsheviks fell upon yet more Sèvres table sets, bronzes and jewellery.

Between them, over the next ten years, Youssoupov's various adversaries plundered the family fortune more or less into extinction. The couple's dress-making business, 'Irfe' – combining the names Irina and Felix – failed and Youssoupov reputedly gave his last stash of money to a destitute refugee, claiming: 'It doesn't matter. I have trust in God.'

Then, in 1932, as if in answer to his prayer, MGM brought out the film *Rasputin and the Empress*. It turned the family's fortune. An American lawyer suggested the couple sue for its damaging portrayal of a character resembling Irina. In the film this character, a 'Princess Natasha', suffers the terrible indignity of being raped by Rasputin. The Youssoupovs won their case and Irina is believed to have walked away with $750,000, or $15 million in today's money.

During the Second World War, Youssoupov, by then in France, was approached by officers sent by Hitler, who had taken it upon himself to offer Youssoupov the Russian throne. But Youssoupov was no more receptive to the Nazis than he had been to the Bolsheviks.

He did not age particularly well. Shortly after the war, on July 29th, 1946, Noel Coward described seeing him at a dinner in the South of France. 'Felix Youssoupov sang really quite sweetly with a guitar. He is made-up to the teeth. I looked at him: a face that must, when young, have been very beautiful but now it is cracking with effort and age.'

In 1949, Youssoupov appeared at an exhibition of Fabergé at Wartskis jewellers in London. He apparently resembled an immaculately tailored wraith, exclaiming grandly: 'My old friend Carl Gustavovich [Fabergé] would have rejoiced to see his wares so diligently set out.' In the 1950s, Youssoupov published two memoirs, *Lost Splendour* and *En Exil*. Sadly, *En Exil*, which began so effusively and poetically with the two-week journey on the *Marlborough*, and would have delighted all the ship's former crew, has never been translated into English. After the publication, history seemed to come full circle as the Soviets again offered to welcome Youssoupov back to Russia. Once more he rejected them.

But if Youssoupov eschewed political life, he thoroughly enjoyed his social life. Like his brother-in-law, Prince Dmitri, he struck up a firm friendship with the Duke and Duchess of Windsor. The only period during which invitations slowed, according to Cecil Beaton, was when he took up with an odiferous holy man, a sort of Mother Martha, who accompanied him everywhere.

He was invited to Menton in the 1960s, where he stayed with a group of White Russians who were entertaining a young Soviet girl from Moscow. She now recalls the White Russians taking a cold interest in her, belabouring her with questions: did she have bread to eat and were there bears roaming the street? She still remembers Youssoupov's piercing eyes.

Youssoupov liked to wear what he claimed was a bullet from Rasputin's dead body on his ring; the bullet is now apparently the property of the poet Yevtushenko. One of his nephews, when asked whether Uncle Felix ever mentioned Rasputin, replied without hesitation: 'My boy, that's all he ever talked about.' As Youssoupov progressed through life, he seemed to pride himself on each additional shocking detail. He told Duff Cooper that Rasputin's performance as a lover was enhanced by three large penile warts. Speculation was rife as to how he could have known; Noel Coward thought he had the answer: 'The truth I think is that Rasputin had a tiny little lech on Youssoupov himself.'

Coward gave a final unflattering description of Youssoupov at one of his later social gatherings, wearing eyeliner, mascara and rouge. He wrote: 'During the dinner, whenever Felix smiled or laughed, the heavy make-up which he wore cracked and kept dropping to the table and into the food.'

Felix Youssoupov died in his bed, aged 80 on September 27th, 1967. His servant Tesphe proved himself tireless and loyal. When Youssoupov had first established himself in Knightsbridge, Tesphe had created a stir by refusing to admit the Dowager and her sister, Queen Alexandra. The Dowager ended up having to threaten him with her umbrella. Woken by the commotion, Youssoupov finally appeared in a dressing gown: 'After apologising for my attire, I explained that Tesphe never disobeyed an order and that, as we had gone to bed very late, we had given him strict instructions not to admit anyone.'

In an equally zealous moment, Tesphe refused to eat for four days when his master developed appendicitis. Youssoupov was operated on in the drawing room of his London flat, partly compensated for his pains with the delivery of a bouquet from Anna Pavlova.

Eventually Tesphe's obsessive qualities led him into a successful career as a healer. Among his patients was a man who thought he was a dog; Tesphe apparently brought about a cure by persuading him to have puppies.

The beauty of Youssoupov's wife, the reticent Irina, proved all too fragile. By her mid-forties, the early travails of life in exile with her Micawber-like husband had taken their toil. She was now 'a frail chain-smoking middle-aged woman with prematurely grey hair'. Her brother, Prince Dmitri, recalled her accompanying their mother's body on a flight from Heathrow to Nice. He was disappointed with her inability to be excited by her first flight: 'it was the first time Irina had been in an aeroplane and she sat away from the window completely oblivious to the flying'.

She died of a heart attack, three years after Youssoupov, on February 26th, 1970.

The Youssoupovs' daughter, little Irina, who had so entranced the *Marlborough* crew, spent her early years with her doting Youssoupov grandparents in a villa in Rome. She was, however, obliged to return to her less transigent parents in Paris after her grandfather suffered a stroke. For all his nonconformist tendencies, Youssoupov deplored his own child's irregular, 'spoilt' behaviour. He was particularly put out when she went under the table and bit the legs of important guests at the grand launch of 'Irfe'.

By 1938, however, Irina had put her feral days well behind her. She married the eminently suitable Nicholas Sheremetiev, whose family had served at the Russian Court for 300 years. During the war she proved to have inherited some of her father's bravado, carrying off a dramatic escape from Italy to Switzerland with her own two-year-old daughter.

Following the tradition of the White Russian exiles, the Sheremetievs remained short of money and, in 1945, Irina was still asking her grandmother Xenia for money. Irina died in 1983.

The Youssoupovs' nanny, the stalwart Miss Zillah Henton, who had tended little Irina so conscientiously, gave an interview to the *Yorkshire Post* in 1936. Now nearly 70, she was the guest of Mr and Mrs Thornton-Berry of Swinthwaite Hall, Wensleydale. Her experiences in Russia had left her virtually penniless and extremely bitter. She had lost all her property and the bulk of her life's savings, deposited, unfortunately, in a bank in St Petersburg. She was scathing about the Bolsheviks, who, she said, 'respected no life, whether high or low, rich or poor'.

The *Yorkshire Post* added its own admonishment to the revolutionaries and their sympathisers in England: 'Miss Henton naturally cannot comprehend the psychology of English people sympathetic with the Russian Communists or of the Soviets who have not yet made a penny restitution of the money belonging to English aliens at the time of the Revolution'.

Miss Henton refused to divulge the name of the aristocrats she had been working for, stating only, cryptically, that they were 'guests of this country'. The identity of her employers would eventually be revealed in several memoirs. But sadly, by the time the courageous 'Henty' was emerging as a public figure, it was too late. Miss Henton died on October 24th, 1940

Youssoupov's parents, the elderly Prince Felix and Princess Zenaide Youssoupov, were among many of the older exiles who, in the early years, fervently believed they would be returning to Russia. Prince Dmitri recalled visiting the couple in 1922 in Italy and seeing a room with an entire floor covered in wine corks; the idea was that these would come in useful when Prince Youssoupov resumed his wine-making business in the Crimea. It was the gift of Crimean wine from 'Prince Youssoupov (sen)' that had gone down so well with the *Marlborough* crew. No less poignant was the Prince's collection of Russian paper money, which he had bought extremely cheaply and which he expected would recover its value when the old regime was reinstated.

In the same spirit of hope, the elderly Prince never quite relinquished his uniform, insisting on wearing his black military boots under his trousers. Every day after lunch, he would be driven to his club, the Caccia, to play bridge. Sitting in the back of the car, he apparently felt less constrained with his boots protruding from the open window.

His wife, the formerly outspoken Zenaide, was subdued by misfortune. Prince Dmitri mentions little of her, beyond her failure even to persuade her husband to shave off the moustaches she so disliked.

The desperate straits of the couple's son Felix through the 1920s did nothing for their spirits. They failed in their attempts to dissuade him from his disastrous trip to America with his jewels. They became increasingly depressed as the likelihood grew that they would never return to Russia or regain any significant aspect of their once glittering life.

The Prince died in 1928, several years before Felix and Irina received their compensation from MGM. The Princess, however, lived to be cheered by her son's windfall and further gratified when she was invited to live with Felix and Irina.

Youssoupov was apparently a conscientious carer for his mother, but, when she eventually died, on November 24th, 1939, she was in a retirement home for Russian exiles. She was buried with her husband at Ste Geneviève des Bois at Essone, outside Paris.

Sofka Dolgorouky, who as an 11-year-old had caught the attention of the *Marlborough* sailors, liked to see herself as a romantic heroine. She would have enjoyed an English childhood in the style of Lorna Doone: wrested from aristocratic parents to be raised by outlaws. Unfortunately, her earliest memories of England were distinctly prosaic: holidays in Margate. Years later, she recalled her disappointment: 'No wild rocks on an unpeopled coast. Here the sands were dry and yellow and strewn with families and the sea came and went in tides. There were donkeys that jogged you sedately a few hundred yards – nothing like the donkey in the

Crimea to whose bare back I would cling as he careered over the grass...

'At eleven every morning all good little boys and girls sat around on seats made in the sand, listened to prayers and sang: "Let the blessed sunshine in". It was very strange.'

While she enjoyed school in London, the holidays were dominated by walks with Granny and games of whist with the dreaded Miss King. Every night she would dream of returning to the Crimea. Her cosseted existence in London filled her with a sort of moral nausea: 'On the next two floors slept Granny, Louise, Olga and nurse, Miss King, Miss New and I. In fact it took seven people to care for three female Dolgoroukys, aged, respectively, sixty-nine, twelve and four.'

Sofka's rebellious streak came to the fore as she enjoyed several wild teenage years in Europe. But in 1931, aged just 23, she seemed to put all turmoil behind her with a suitable marriage to a fellow White Russian, Leo Zinovieff. The marriage, attended by Grand Duchess Xenia, was respectably followed by the birth of two sons.

Sadly, the boys were soon fighting an ever losing battle for the attention of their mother, who was constantly distracted by other commitments. First came her job with Laurence Olivier, which entailed her sharing a bed with a pet lemur called Tony. Secondly and more controversially came a growing passion for left-wing causes, or, as she preferred, 'mildly pink activities'. It was probably a relief to her in-laws when Leo and Sofka divorced. In 1937 she married Grey Skipwith and the couple had Patrick, whose hold on his parents was so slight that they left him with the milkman's mother-in-law, while they travelled with a Cossack circus.

After war had been declared, Sofka, perhaps ill-advisedly,

travelled to Paris, where she was arrested and put into an internment camp because of her British citizenship. The end of the war saw her widowed and ready to embrace a lifestyle and ideology which would put her forever at variance with her fellow White Russians. Kyril Zinovieff put it peremptorily: 'Very soon after the war she joined the Communist Party... she ceased to exist for the other refugees – on the *Marlborough* or not. Communists and refugees are completely divided. It would be the same as Jews fraternising with Nazis.'

She took a job with a new communist travel company, Progressive Tours, and happily took factory workers and trade union officials around the palaces in which she had grown up. Such was her commitment that she was watched by MI5 and even had her phone tapped. If MI5 gleaned little from their investigations, they were on to her espousal of free love, labelling her 'oversexed'.

But Sofka would not be deterred by MI5 any more than she was by Stalin. As she insisted: 'The evils of Stalin should not be allowed to detract from the ideals of Communism.' She was over 70 before she was persuaded to live in her own house. Her youngest son, the neglected Patrick, bought her a house in Shepherds Bush after inheriting money from the Skipwiths on his 21st birthday. Two of her sons, Patrick and Peter, led predictably rackety lives but the third, Ian, confounded her by becoming a bank manager.

What the officers of the *Marlborough* would have thought of their little passenger's espousal of Communism can only be imagined. The sailor Lionel Vanstone, who had acted as server at the Easter service, wrote to her saying he had never forgotten the affect the national anthem had upon the Russians: 'I remember how the playing of the Russian national anthem affected both the nobility aboard the

Marlborough and those at Halki.' Sofka may not have relished his image of the refugees' misery as they wept over the demise of the monarchy.

She ended her days in Cornwall with a fellow Communist called Jack King and died in February 1994, aged 86. After her death she was given a medal by the Israeli embassy for those who had risked their lives helping Jews during the war.

Sofka's colourful nanny, Miss King, stayed with the Dolgoroukys for several years after they settled in England. Perhaps feeling spurned by her fellow humans, Miss King became obsessed with the Dolgoroukys' dog and fellow *Marlborough* passenger, Pupsik. She began to demand special food and privileges for Pupsik, now aged and riddled with eczema.

Her nose was put out of joint by the appointment of the second nanny, appropriately named Miss New – employed to look after Sofka's cousin, the four-year-old Olga, who had accompanied her on the *Marlborough*. Miss King and Miss New were soon at daggers drawn. As Sofka recalled: 'Miss King was convinced that Miss New was trying to poison both her and Pupsik. Miss New was certain that Miss King was out of her mind and only waiting for a chance to knife her.'

It must have been a cause for general celebration when an excuse arose to dismiss Miss King. The moment came in the mid-1920s when Miss King discovered Sofka cavorting with a young admirer in a garden in Florence. While the disgrace was Sofka's, it was deemed easier to dispose of the witness. Another job was immediately found for Miss King. She duly left, as Sofka recalled: 'but not before flinging things at my head and prophesying that I should come to a gloomy and immoral end.'

As for the Dulbers, the majestic Grand Duke Nicholas

initially kept the resolve he had made on the *Marlborough* to keep out of public life. But he could not avoid an unofficial role as a prominent head of the Romanov family.

In 1920, it fell to him to deal with the Sokolov document, in which details were given of the first full investigation into the murders of the Tsar and his family. Nikolasha gave the document to lawyers to check its authenticity. He wrote to Xenia: 'Then it will all have to be sent to your august Mother. It can be done only through you, as you alone can prepare her for these minutes – a nightmare that cannot be described – if the investigation confirms the legal authenticity. May God help you and all of us to bear such a heavy trial which has been sent on to us from above.'

Three years later, he supported the august Dowager in her opposition to Grand Duke Kyril's claim to the throne. In the wake of Kyril's manifesto, Nikolasha issued his own. The future aim, he argued, should be to re-establish law in Russia without stipulating any form of government. He disputed Grand Duke Kyril's claim to the throne not least because Kyril's mother had not adopted the Orthodox faith upon her marriage.

Throughout the 1920s, Nikolasha was pestered by Russians begging him to take action against the Bolsheviks. These were mostly immigrants, but others had travelled all the way from Soviet Russia to see him. He cannot have failed to be moved by the arrival of icon-wielding deputations.

His hopes may have been raised as he heard tales of peasants killing Communists or read *Pravda* articles complaining of 'a dangerous increase of monarchist activity in the country'. In the end he could not resist the continuing campaign. He agreed to become the leader of an organisation called the Russian Nationalist Committee. It is hard to know to what extent he believed the Bolsheviks could be overthrown. But it was estimated at the time that he would have had some 100,000 supporters, including military refugees and the Union of Russian Officers Abroad. A *Daily Telegraph* report, from its Belgrade correspondent, while welcoming his decision, was slightly sniffy in tone: 'The Grand Duke Nicholas... has at last cast aside political inactivity and put himself at the head of a new union to resist the Russian Bolsheviks.'

Grand Duke Nicholas ended his days in a tiny villa in Paris. According to the *Morning Post*, he refused to see foreigners on principle. There was just one exception, an Englishman, Commander Oliver Locker-Lampson, who had served under him in the Caucasus. Locker-Lampson, a barrister and Tory MP, founded the blue-shirted 'Sentinels of The Empire', whose stated aim was to 'peacefully fight Bolshevism and clear out the Reds!' He later created controversy by claiming, during the Youssoupovs' MGM trial, that he himself had been invited to murder Rasputin. In 1930 he wrote a paeon to Hitler in the *Daily Mirror*: 'The temperature in the room rises in his presence. He makes the humblest fellow feel twice the man.'

Grand Duke Nicholas fell ill with pneumonia a month before his death, aged 72, in 1929 at Cap d'Antibes. Funeral masses were sung in all the Russian churches in France. *Le Temps* declared him: 'a model of uprightness of loyalty and magnanimity'. With all his disdain for foreigners, he would have been pleased to know that at least two of the officers on the *Marlborough* carefully conserved his obituaries.

Nikolasha's wife, Anastasia, who had once been so handy with the broom, seems to have kept a low profile. Obituaries stated simply that she had been one of five Montenegrin princesses famed for their beauty; she had been sister of the Queen of Italy and had married, first, Prince George Romanovsky,

Duke of Leuchtenberg, in 1889, then Grand Duke Nicholas, in 1907. She died in Cap d'Antibes in November 1935.

Grand Duke Nicholas's brother, Peter, spent his early years in exile in Antibes, with his wife, Militsa, his children Roman and Marina, and a few loyal servants: the remnants, as his grandsons put it, of Dulber. He lived quietly, devoting most of his time to painting religious pictures. He had been ill for some time before he died, aged 67, in 1931.

Five years after Grand Duke Peter's death, his widow, Militsa, moved with her family to Lucca, in Italy. The family had been invited by her sister, the Queen of Italy. But any hope Militsa might have had of enjoying a quiet life was thwarted by the outbreak of the Second World War. Her psychic gifts proved of little use as she repeatedly failed to avoid the Germans during the occupation of Rome. She was threatened with deportation back to Russia and was eventually reduced to hiding in a convent before fleeing to the Vatican. Just after the war, in 1946, the family moved to Egypt, apparently travelling on an Italian cruiser used to bring Italian prisoners of war back from India and Kenya. Grand Duchess Militsa died in Egypt in 1951.

Two years after his escape on the *Marlborough*, the couple's son, Prince Roman, married another distinguished White Russian, Countess Prascovia, then aged just 20. The young couple settled near Roman's parents at Cap d'Antibes, where they established, poignantly, an entirely pre-revolutionary Russian way of life. Presumably at some inconvenience, they insisted on sticking to the Julian calendar. They educated their two sons privately, according to the traditional Russian school curriculum. Finally, they converted one of their rooms into a chapel and installed their own priest. Father Zossima, whose name echoed that of Dostoyevsky's charismatic priest in *The Brothers Karamazov*, completed the couple's tribute to 19th-century Russia.

Roman and his family moved with his mother, Militsa, to Italy in 1936. They managed to avoid her experience of being harried by Germans by establishing themselves in a flat owned by a Swiss. They accompanied Militsa to Egypt, returning to Italy after her death. Prince Roman died in Italy in 1978.

In April 1992, Roman's son, Prince Nicholas, became head of the Romanov family. He visited Russia for the first time in June 1992. In the early 1990s, he and his brother published their father's memoir in Danish, *At the Court of the Last Tsar*, in which fond tributes are paid to the *Marlborough* crew, particularly First Lieutenant Pridham.

In 1998, Prince Nicholas led the Romanov family at the historic funerals in St Petersburg of the Tsar and his family and four retainers. Prince Nicholas kept the ring with a sapphire that his grandfather, Grand Duke Peter, had tried to saw off during the family's captivity at Dulber. The idea had been that the sapphire would be kept and sold separately. The ring still bears the notch left by the teeth of the saw.

Roman's sister, Princess Marina, married another distinguished White Russian, Prince Nicholas Galitzine. Prince Nicholas died in 1974. Marina in 1981.

Captain Charles Johnson remained in the Navy, becoming Commander in Chief of the Mediterranean Fleet and retiring an Admiral in 1930. Several of his competitive brothers also distinguished themselves. Alongside Captain Arthur there was Frank, awarded one of the first DFCs after fighting on the Western Front, and Sir Gordon, appointed Commissioner of Delhi. Admiral Charles Johnson was stationed in Malta before settling with his wife Lucy in Leixlip Castle, County Kildare.

Many of Johnson's possessions and papers are missing, perhaps because the couple had no children. However, the epaulets and buttons from his Naval blazer are carefully tended by his nephew, Michael Johnson, who has had the buttons sewn onto his blazer. These, along with the *Marlborough* telescope, a sword, and the cigarette box given to the Captain by the Dowager, are kept in the house in Witney that Michael shares with his wife Helen.

One of the few cuttings Michael has retained is an article from the *Johannesburg Star* commemorating the 50th anniversary of the Russian Revolution in 1967. In the article, Michael is pictured with 'Uncle Charlie's' cigarette box and medals. There is one medal missing; as Michael adds: 'I think his wife (Lucy) was responsible for the loss of the larger special Russian medal.'

The family is mystified as to how Charlie's precious letters from the King became public. Michael says he saw letters quoted at the back of Pridham's memoir: 'That's when I became suspicious.'

The Johnsons clearly feel that the Captain's letters have been somehow devalued by being disseminated. But the simple answer is that, like the photographs, copies of the letters were distributed liberally among the sailors. Perhaps this was the most effective way for the taciturn Captain Johnson to thank his men. Admiral Charles Johnson died on June 26th 1930. He is buried in Ireland.

Following the rescue mission and in recognition of his success as governor, for a week, of the Turkish town of Gemlik, Commander 'Tom' Fothergill received the Order of St Anne's medal from King George V. In 1920 he left the *Marlborough*, having served on the ship for six years. Soon after, he married Lucy Pusey and joined the Reserve Fleet.

During the Second World War, he was called up and sent to Brazil to re-route cargo ships. On the way, his ship was torpedoed and he was at sea in a sailing boat for nine days before being rescued. When he finally returned to Camberley, he was greeted at the station by his imperturbable wife, Lucy. Her first concern was his appearance: 'Where did you get that awful suit?' After the war, he was appointed Naval Officer in Larne, Northern Ireland, in charge of training captains of escorts to cross the Atlantic.

While Tom Fothergill seemed at first slightly reluctant to involve himself in the Romanovs' venture on the *Marlborough*, his essential goodheartedness got the better of him. The extent to which he was beguiled by the Romanovs and, after two weeks, bereft at their departure, is clear from the extensive archive he collected of photographs, news stories and letters.

In the end, Fothergill clearly viewed the rescue as a defining moment of his life. For all his breezy stoicism, it was he, of all the officers, who succumbed to a fondness which extended to the ship herself. Rivalling his Romanov archive is a collection of HMS *Marlborough* cuttings and artefacts. One cutting, from 1932, announces that she is to be decommissioned. Upon spotting the article, Tom Fothergill immediately wrote asking whether he could have the ship's bell. Sadly, it had already been given to Marlborough College.

He treasured photographs of the *Marlborough* bear, which took up residence outside his cabin shortly after the departure of the Romanovs. 'Bruno' nipped sailors' toes as they scrubbed the deck in bare feet. When Bruno swam off the ship, he was often unable to find his way back and the cry would go up: 'Who's got *Marlborough*'s bear?' Bruno was finally installed in London Zoo.

Fothergill ended up acquiring the *Marlborough*'s model

The *Marlborough* bear, Bruno, who nipped sailors' toes as
they scrubbed the deck in bare feet

steam-train set. At the end of the First World War, Captain
Johnson said the first officer to have a son would get the
set, complete with green express engine and two-foot carriages. In 1922, Tom Fothergill had the first son: Christopher
Fothergill still remembers soda water bottles at the ready to
extinguish engine fires.

Commander Henry 'Tom' Fothergill died in 1963 aged 81.

Christopher – also a Naval Commander – and his wife
Linda follow the news of the *Marlborough*'s successors. The
couple recently attended the commissioning of the new
HMS *Marlborough* on the Thames; also attending were the
headmaster of Marlborough College and the Duke of
Marlborough. In their home near Rugby, they carefully
maintain Commander Fothergill's archives, his St Anne's
medal and, most precious of all, his fond letters to Rhoda, or
'Punch'. 'Punch' and 'the others' – as he referred to them –
never married. As Linda says, there was just one sister, Ada,
who got away: 'There's a photograph of her on a camel.'

Vice-Admiral Sir Francis Pridham spent the rest of his

professional life in the Navy. He had an illustrious career, becoming Captain of the *Marlborough* in 1922 and, 14 years later, Captain of the HMS *Hood*. During the Second World War, he was made Vice-Admiral. One of the family's favourite stories has it that, in 1943, the Navy wanted to send him to Washington as the Senior Naval Representative. Churchill immediately objected, growling: 'Pridham must stay.'

His granddaughter, Sarah Padwick, remembers him as the embodiment of a traditional Victorian: restrained and distant. But equally Victorian was his compulsion to keep a soul-searching diary and, eventually, to write his moving memoir, *Close of a Dynasty*. 'Emotions are easier on paper,' as Sarah explains cheerfully.

In fact, Pridham's outer nod to conformity was belied by an unconventional streak. His lifelong commitment to Anglicanism was supplemented by experiments with faith-healing to deal with painful bouts of arthritis. And there is no doubting his susceptibility to the Romanovs' story. Like Fothergill, he maintained a collection of cuttings and photographs of the Romanovs. These were carefully conserved alongside his more obviously precious jewelled eggs, religiously worn by members of the Pridham family every Easter Sunday. Upon his return to England, Pridham had one of the Romanov jewels attached to a watch chain which, he was proud to say, he wore constantly.

While most of the *Marlborough* officers were captivated by the Romanovs, Pridham was the only one to establish lifelong relationships. When the Dowager died in 1928, Grand Duchess Xenia took on her role of godmother to little Joan Marie Pridham, by then aged nine.

It was Xenia who encouraged her erstwhile 'Job' to write his memoir, which remains the most detailed account of the surviving Romanovs' first faltering steps into exile. She wrote a moving letter of appreciation, which Pridham included as a foreword. Her words are lent additional weight by being reproduced simply in her handwriting: 'It is with great interest that I have read your book, which revives so many poignant memories. I always think with heartfelt gratitude of the kindness shown by all hands on the *Marlborough* to my mother, the Empress Marie, to myself and my family on that fateful journey. Grand Duchess Xenia.' The pair enjoyed a respectful friendship into old age, perhaps each relishing the memory of their roles on the *Marlborough*: the gallant British officer on a mission to save the beguiling Grand Duchess.

Pridham's description of their relationship in his own foreward was, characteristically, both formal and moving: 'During the remainder of her life, it was my respectful privilege to become accepted by the Grand Duchess Xenia as a close friend... My wife and I and also my youngest daughter Joan were frequently received by the Grand Duchess while she was living in Hampton Court. She died there in April 1960, aged 85, retaining to the last that sublime gift of gracious charm combined with regal dignity. I carry in my mind a picture of the Grand Duchess that we often saw – a small, fragile and still beautiful old lady standing alone at the head of her staircase blowing a kiss to us as we turned and made her a parting bow.' Vice-Admiral Sir Francis Pridham died in 1975. His ashes were committed to the sea off Portland.

His book, *Close of a Dynasty*, stood the test of time; his grandson, Lieutenant-Commander David Gould, recently collected £300 in royalties which he then divided between the Sea Cadet Units of the *Marlborough* and *Hood*. Less happily,

Gould decided to show the family's prized jewelled eggs to John Benjamin on the *Antiques Roadshow*: he revealed that the eggs were not Fabergé. The family pride was amply restored, however, by Benjamin's excitement over their provenance. 'His eyes gleamed,' reported Gould.

Alongside Pridham's archive, his granddaughter Sarah Padwick keeps at her home in Devizes a keepsake perhaps more precious for not being a gift from a Romanov; the fearsome dagger presented to Pridham by the Dowager's Cossack.

Chief Petty Officer Sidney Webber, who had formed such a merry friendship with Princess 'Ice-a-Creama', didn't get home to Plymouth until late 1920, by which time his whole family had succumbed to Spanish flu. As his son explained in a letter to the BBC in the 1970s: 'my father actually arrived in the house to find myself aged nine and a half and my grandmother the only two people capable of moving around the house. I had been up a couple of days, my mother got up that day and my grandfather was getting up next day, so stories of the cruise had to take a back seat until things were more or less back to normal... When the rescue was over my father saw no more of the refugees but he said that apparently some were going to Canada. Whether the Princess told him that, I don't know. For some years we think he was hoping to hear from "Ice a Creama" to know she was safe and well but he left the Navy in 1922 and 1926...' (presumably the beginnings of the Depression) '...made us think of our survival and worry about the future to the exclusion of all else!' Chief Petty Officer Webber died in 1942.

Marine Phillips, who had been so affected by the sight of the Dowager leaving the Crimea, talked endlessly of his *Marlborough* mission. His daughter now says: 'He nearly drowned us with all this stories. But you don't take it in when you're young.' He died in 1972.

Seaman Joseph Albiston, who had been given a gun by Princess Marina, served in the Second World War and spent four years as a Japanese POW. He used to like talking to his grandchildren about the *Marlborough* bear. His grandson remembers being told about the bear coming down into the mess and eating jam sandwiches. During bathing sessions, Bruno would sit on the end of the metal ladder with his feet in the water and prevent the sailors coming back on ship. Albiston kept Princess Marina's gun for the rest of his life. It is now kept by his grandson in France. He died in 1985 aged 90.

'Robbie' Roberts, the server at the *Marlborough* Easter services, was moved, years later, to see a bridal portrait of Princess Sofka Dolgorouky. He had been working as a gardener for the portrait painter when he saw the picture. He retained vivid memories of the 11-year-old Sofka and her English governess (Miss King).

George Gravestock, who had picked a rose from the Crimea for his fiancée Ethel, always kept a picture of HMS *Marlborough* hanging above the couple's bed. Charles Wakeling's grandson, Michael, rescued some 20 photographs of the Imperial Family on the *Marlborough*. They had been deposited in a coal-hole and were due to be thrown out. Michael Wakeling describes his grandfather as a cheerful man who never talked about his Naval career but retained his ship's steward's skill of making cocktails – including one comprising gin and rum called 'Cholera'.

As for the ship herself, shortly after completing her mission to rescue the Romanovs, the *Marlborough* had the distinction of receiving one of Nelson's dinner plates. The plate was awarded to her in June 1919 for rendering herself 'conspicuous amongst her gallant comrades'. An accompanying certificate read: 'The Navy League trusts that you will recognise it as an expression of gratitude to the Glorious Fleet, of which your ship is so distinguished a representative.'

The ship flourished for some time and, in 1926, she was refitted and transferred to the Atlantic Fleet; but within six years her fortunes had turned and, in compliance with the Washington Treaty, she was scrapped.

Of service to the end, she was felled in Plymouth in June 1932 as part of an experiment to gauge the extent of damage caused by explosions. Or, as Fothergill's *Morning Post* recorded more precisely: 'Before being sent [to the shipbreakers yard] she was used for experimental explosive tests to obtain data regarding the effects of internal explosions in warships.' In the 1930s the figurehead of the *Marlborough* was preserved at Portsmouth Dockyard.

The ship's bell was presented to Marlborough College in November 1933 by three former pupils who were or had been officers on HMS *Marlborough*: Paymaster Eric Bramley Elstob, Surgeon Lieutenant John Joyce Keevil and Thomas Nevil Masterman. It now stands 12 feet off the ground in the dining hall of the college and is regularly rung by senior prefects.

On April 11th, 2009, Sergei Stafeev, who describes himself as 'a philosopher more than a historian' and his friend Sergey Sardyko, director of the 'Yalta Friends Club', organised an anniversary to commemorate the departure of the Romanovs from Yalta. Two months before, plans were going awry and Sergei was in a panic. As he wrote in an e-mail: 'The time is very short now, we spent a lot of time for burocratical [sic] paperwork and blah-blah, also taking endorsements in GorSovet, architectural department, etc etc...'

Though in the end he succeeded in organising a plaque,

the wording had to be amended several times. The original inscription read: 'On April 11 1919 the British battleship HMS *Marlborough* departed from the Yalta roadstead taking away into for ever exile of the survived members of Russian Imperial Family of Romanovs, among them the Dowager Empress Marie Feodorovna.'

The crew of the *Marlborough*, particularly Pridham and Fothergill, would have been gratified by this tribute from the people of Yalta. Most of the passengers would also have appreciated any effort to mark their momentous rescue. But sadly, or perhaps predictably, the enjoyment of the Romanovs themselves would have been tainted by a faux pas. The generally recognised head of the family is Roman's son, Prince Nicholas, but the plaque was unveiled by a representative of Grand Duchess Maria, whose grandfather's claims to the title had so infuriated both the Dowager and the Grand Duke Nicholas in 1924.

The Yalta Friends' Club would have been mortified at their generous gesture backfiring. But perhaps there is poetry in the idea of all 17 *Marlborough* Romanovs – even the Black Sisters – looking down aghast, united finally in disapproval.

Photograph of HMS *Marlborough*, signed by several
of the Russian passengers

BIBLIOGRAPHY

Arthur, Max: *The True Glory, The Royal Navy 1914-1939* (London, Hodder & Stoughton, 1997)

Ashmore, Vice Admiral Leslie H: *Forgotten Flotilla* (Portsmouth Manuscript Press, The Royal Navy Submarine Museum, 2001)

Belyakova, Zoya: *The Romanovs, The Way It Was* (St Petersburg, Ego Publishers, 2000)

Clarke, William: *The Lost Fortune of the Tsars* (London, Orion 2000)

Cook, Andrew: *To Kill Rasputin* (The History Press, 2010)

Crawford, Michael and Natasha: *The Life And Love of the Last Tsar of Russia* (London, Weidenfeld & Nicolson 1997)

Faber, Toby: *Fabergé's Eggs* (London, Macmillan, 2007)

Friederika, Marie Sophie: *Dagmar, the Russian Empress Marie Fiodorovna* (St Petersburg, Abris Publishers, 2006)

Galitzine, Prince VE, ADC to Grand Duke Nicholas Nicholaivitch 1915-1919 (Belij Gorod)

Hall, Coryne: *Little Mother of Russia, A Biography of Empress Marie Feodorovna* (London, Shepheard-Walwyn, 1999)

HI & RH Grand Duchess George: *A Romanov Diary* (New York, Atlantic Publications, 1988)

Marias, Javier: *Written Lives* (Edinburgh, Canongate, 2006)

Massie, Robert K: *Nicholas and Alexandra* (New York: Atheneum, 1967)

Mengden, Countess Zinaide: *Memoirs of Countess Zinaide Mengden* (Copenhagen, H.Hagerup, 1943)

Nabokov, Vladimir: *Speak, Memory* (Middlesex, Penguin Books, 1966)

Neerbek, Hans: *Tikhon, The Tsar's Nephew* (Sweden Royal Books, 2005)

Payn, Graham and Morley, Sheridan: *The Noel Coward Diaries* (Cambridge, MA, Da Capo Press, 2000)

Perry, John Curtis; Pleshakov, Constantine: *The Flight of the Romanovs* (New York, Basic Books, 1999)

Pridham, Sir Francis: *Close of a Dynasty* (London, Allan Wingate, 1956)

Quennell, Peter: *A Lonely Business, A Self-Portrait of James Pope-Hennessey* (London, Weidenfeld & Nicolson, 1981)

Rappaport, Helen: *Ekaterinburg* (London, Hutchinson, 2008)

Radzinsky, Edvard: *Rasputin The Last Word* (London, Phoenix, 2002)

Romanov, Roman Petrovich: *Am Hof des Letzten Tsaren* (Munich, Piper, 2006)

Skipwith, Sofka: *Sofka, The Autobiography of a Princess* (London, Rupert Hart-Davis, 1968)

Sollohub, Edith: *The Russian Countess* (Exeter, Impress Books, 2009)

Stoeckl, Baroness Agnes de: *Not All Vanity* (London, John Murray, 1950)

Stone, Norman and Glenny, Michael: *The Other Russia* (London, Faber and Faber, 1990)

Tsarina Alexandra: *Last Diary of* (New Haven, CT, Yale University, 1997)

Van der Kiste, John & Hall, Coryne: *Xenia Sister of Nicholas II* (Stroud, Sutton Publishing, 2004)

Ulstrup, Preben: *Empress Dagmar's Captivity in the Crimea* (Copenhagen, Gyldendal, 2005)

Updike, John: *The Maples Stories* (Everyman, 2009)

Yachik, TK: *Next to the Empress, Memoirs of a Cossack*

Youssoupov, Felix: *Lost Splendour* (London, Jonathan Cape, 1953)

Youssoupov, Felix: *En Exil* (Paris, Librairie Plon, 1954)

Youssoupov, Felix: *Rasputin – His Malignant Influence And His Assassination* (London, Jonathan Cape, 1934)

Zeepvat, Charlotte: *From Cradle To Crown* (Stroud, Sutton Publishing, 2006)

Zinovieff, Elizabeth: *A Princess Remembers, A Russian Life* (YN Galitzine & J Ferrand, 1997)

Zinovieff, Sofka: *Red Princess, A Revolutionary Life* (London, Granta Books, 2007)

Other Sources

The National Archives, Kew; Churchill College, Cambridge; Imperial War Museum; unpublished memoir of Prince Dmitri, property of Penny Galitzine; unpublished diary of Rear Admiral Denham Maurice Turner Bedford (original diaries held by Patricia Beeny (née Bedford)); Anthony Summers' collection accumulated for *The File On The Tsar* by Tom Mangold and Anthony Summers (Victor Gollancz, 1976) and a BBC documentary, including interviews with Francis Pridham,

Michael Laing and Mr Douglas, and letters from crew members of the HMS *Marlborough* and HMS *Lord Nelson*: Phillips, Mitchell, Webber, Parker, Ottaway, Wilson, Golding, Bennett and Sullivan; *Imperial Russian Journal*: Empress Alexandra Feodorovna (Pavlovsk Press, Summer, 1995); *What Happened to the Empress*: Robert Ingham (printed at St Joseph's Ins., Hamrun, Malta, 1949); *A Nation's Praise*: AE Abela (Valletta, Progress Press, 1994); Royal Danish Arsenal Museum brochure (exhibition: January to December 2003); *Treasures of Russia - Imperial Gifts* (exhibition: Amalienborg Palace, Copenhagen, 2002); newspapers: *Daily Malta Chronicle, Sunday Times of Malta, Yorkshire Post, Morning Post, The Sunday Times, The Times, Daily Telegraph.*

ACKNOWLEDGEMENTS:

I'm particularly grateful for their kindness and unstinting help
to Vice Admiral Sir Francis Pridham's grandchildren, Sarah
Padwick and Lt Commander David Gould; Commander Fothergill's
son and daughter-in-law, Commander Christopher
and Linda Fothergill; Admiral Johnson's nephew and niece,
Michael and Helen Johnson; and several relations of crew
members, including Mike Wakeling, John Coram, Marion
Allen, Richard M Johnson, Elisabeth Morse and Mike Webber.

Also to Prince Dmitri's granddaughter, Penny Galitzine; Prince
Vassily's friend, Albert Bartridge; Princess Sofka's granddaughter, Sofka
Zinovieff; and her great uncle, Kyril Zinovieff.

Anthony Summers and Robbyn Swan put me up in Ireland. Philip and
Sonia Goodman, who knew passengers from HMS *Marlborough*, were
extremely helpful.

Otherwise I'm grateful for constructive e-mail exchanges and
correspondences with William Clarke, Greg King, Charlotte Zeepvat,
Ian Shapiro, Jenny Carr, Marion Wynn, Janet Ashton, Joanna Tan,
Tobie Mathew, Susan Sykes, George Gainsburgh, Richard Davies,
John Gooding, Rev Deacon Andrew Bond, Marina Lermontov, Masha
Lees, Edward Snow and Sergei Stafeev. Charles Miller supplied the
unpublished diary of Rear Admiral Bedford. Helen Molchanoff and
Coryne Hall provided invaluable initial support. Terry Rogers,
archivist of Marlborough College, supplied details of the ship's bell.

The Dowager's diary was painstakingly translated from the Old
Danish by Karen Roth. Other translations from French and German
are my own.

The book is dependent on its photographs. For these I would like
to thank Commander Christopher Fothergill, Lt Commander David
Gould, Sarah Padwick, Mike Wakeling, Marion Allen and Penny
Galitzine.

Finally, I am especially grateful to Sue Woolmans, without whose
tireless research this book could not have been written.

And to my husband Craig who willingly joined me on the voyage.